E S S E N T I A L
BUSHFIRE
SAFETY TIPS

THIRD EDITION

THIS HOUSE
WAS
ACTIVELY
DEFENDED.

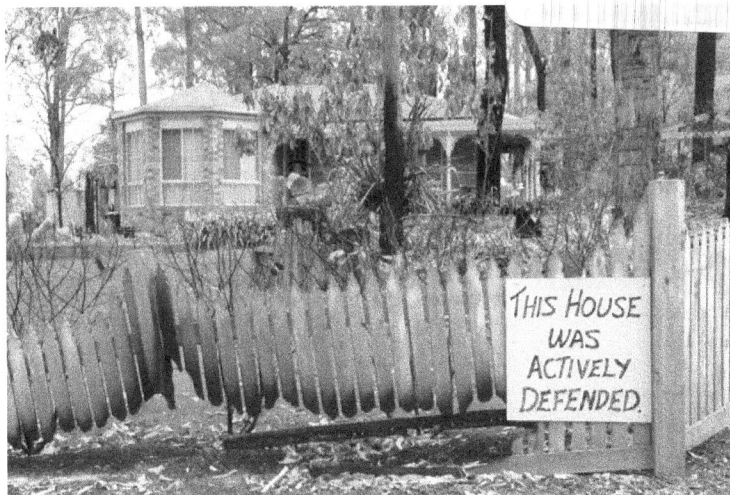

Joan Webster OAM

Essential Bushfire Safety Tips

Published by Melliodora Publishing October 2021

First edition of *Essential Bushfire Safety Tips* published by Random House 2001

Third edition of *Essential Bushfire Safety Tips* previously published by CSIRO Publishing 2012

MELLI⬤DORA
PUBLISHING

Published by Melliodora Publishing
16 Fourteenth Street Hepburn
Victoria Australia 3461

melliodora.com
hello@melliodorapublishing.com

A catalogue record for this work is available from the National Library of Australia

Cover photograph: Calum Robertson

Title page photograph: Katherine Seppings; the home of Travis and Denise Griffith, Kinglake, Victoria, Australia.

ISBN: 978-0-6483442-7-8

Praise for Joan Webster OAM

"*Essential Bushfire Safety Tips* was essential reading and definitely saved lives and property in Kangaroo Valley on January 4, 2020. Kangaroo Valley is now, arguably, the best example of a prepared community. Much of our preparedness was on account of your book *Essential Bushfire Safety Tips* and talking to you."

> *Capt Matthew Gray Chairman,*
> *Community Bushfire Planning Committee,*
> *Kangaroo Valley, NSW.*

"Joan Webster's book *Essential Bushfire Safety Tips* not only comprehensively covers a plethora of great ideas for preparing yourselves and your home for a bushfire, but it really helped us visualise what would happen during the various phases of the fire. The chapter 'What to do when bushfire threatens' really spelt out in clear and understandable terms what to expect, and what we needed to do and when."

> *Paul Cooper and Maureen Bell,*
> *Kangaroo Valley, NSW*

"Your books are used by our RFS (Rural Fire Service) officers and residents and were the means of saving many homes in the Black Summer bushfires, 2020"

> *Seb King, Gosford, NSW*

"I gave my daughter a copy of your book before the Kilmore East fires, 2009, and they saved their own place and the house behind them. Your advice has, and will, save lives"

> *Antoinette Birkenbeil,*
> *Chewton Bushlands, Victoria*

"Though *Essential Bushfire Safety Tips* is written for Australia, its lessons are universal."

> *The Natural Hazards Observer,*
> *Natural Hazards Center,*
> *University of Colorado-Boulder*

"Thank you for everything you have done for all of us in the wildland urban interface. Needless to say, your work has had a tremendous and very beneficial impact over here."

Adrian Cameron,
Designer, Training Program for Volunteers, Fire Safe Council,
Nevada County, California, USA

"Your efforts have saved many lives already and your publications have become classics that will continue to help us while the threat of death by fire escalates. *Essential Bushfire Safety Tips* is packed with valuable information in a form allowing quick reference. Your books are the most complete and authoritative in the Southern Hemisphere and probably the world."

Dr Barry Richardson, Phd.,
Jeeralang Junction via Churchill, Victoria,
Founder of FireAway

"Like all Joan Webster OAM's information published, to know these facts and act on them will save your life and the lives of others around you, including animals, if you're caught in the grasp of a fire."

DART (Disaster Animal Response Team Australia)

"No-one else has so succinctly and accurately delivered the science in an accessible way with practical actions that anyone can follow, as in *Essential Bushfire Safety Tips*".

Virginia Solomon, Trainer - Horticulture and Permaculture
Landscape Designer, Eltham, Victoria

"In my opinion, *Essential Bushfire Safety Tips* is the best written on the subject of how to prepare oneself, their home and to be acutely aware of the area they live in. The researched and accurate information supplied in the book can only contribute to the saving of lives and property.

John Peacock, ex-CFA, Belgrave, Victoria

Foreword

Bushfire is part of the Australian environment. Before European settlement, fire was widespread during the dry seasons in most parts of Australia. Prior to establishment of the state forestry services and volunteer bushfire brigades in the early 1900s, there was little capacity to check bushfire, apart from burning off early in the dry season around valued assets just as the indigenous Australians had done for centuries. People who lived in the country were familiar with fire, used fire and knew how to protect themselves from uncontrolled fire.

As Australia developed agriculture and towns, people of European heritage saw fire as totally undesirable and purely destructive not only to agricultural assets but also to the natural environment. Legislation restricting the lighting of fires and, more recently, fear of litigation from fire escapes has dramatically reduced the amount of burning off on private property during mild weather. Today, particularly in southern Australia, our population is largely urbanised and the use of fire in the countryside is being more and more restricted. Vigilant bushfire brigades have also reduced the areas burnt in mild weather so that many landholders rely on them for protection and have little knowledge or experience of fire whatsoever.

Despite our best efforts, bushfires will be ignited by lightning, accident or arson. Over the possible range of fire intensity, our ability to suppress fire is puny. This means that fire will start and spread unchecked during dangerous fire weather and people in its path will be confronted with phenomena of which they may have no previous experience.

Fire is a chemical reaction that gives off heat and light. Australian scientists have led the world in understanding bushfire behaviour and we know a lot about it. We know it is highly variable because fire responds to variation in wind, vegetation and topography – but it obeys the laws of physics. Hydrocarbon gases from heated dry vegetation combine with oxygen and burn as a diffusion flame which has known characteristics of temperature, radiation and convective flux. Knowing these properties allows us to predict a fire's behaviour and take action to survive and protect property.

Bushfire maintains its energy by continually moving into new fuel – the fuel is the only factor we can manage, to stop fire and reduce its impact. Bushfire fuel is all around us, even in built-up suburban areas. Knowing what fuel is important, how it burns and what can be done to reduce its flammability is absolutely critical to surviving bushfire in the Australian countryside.

In compiling this book Joan Webster OAM has drawn on consultations with fire scientists over many years. The information is set out in straightforward point form. I urge all Australians to be aware that they may encounter a bushfire when living in, or simply travelling through, the countryside. We should all plan well in advance what we need to do to protect our family and assets.

NP Cheney PSM
Former Head, CSIRO Bushfire Behaviour and Management

Contents

Bushfire Danger Aspects

- Intensity of fire
- Flame height, distance, exposure time
- Amount of skin exposed, flimsy clothes

Bushfire Threat Distinctions

- Bush/grass, mild/intense, sudden/forecast
- Topography, vegetation, housing density
- House style, garden type, preparation

Bushfire Threat Modifiers

- Weather on the day
- Vulnerability/safety of houses
- Preparation, personal reactions

Life Threats

- Heat: radiant, superheated air, steam
- Smoke and toxic gases
- Dehydration

Life Savers

- Protective clothes, pure wool blanket
- Nose cover
- Drinking enough water

Survival Blanket

- Must be pure wool; must be dry
- Radiant heat can't penetrate
- Embers can't ignite or melt

Smoke/Toxic Gas Protection

- Masks that filter 0.01 μm
- Wet towel
- In-house fittings of natural fibres

Home Vulnerable Areas

- Roof/ceiling space
- Windows
- Subfloor

Home Destroyers

- Embers: most usual
- Flames: not usual
- Radiant heat: rarely

Home Savers

- Ember proofing
- Garden preparation
- Enough equipment, reserve water

Home Defence
- Limit water use until embers fall
- Limit activity to dousing embers
- Never attack approaching flames

Sheltering Safely
- Close windows, doors, seal gaps
- Wear protective clothing
- Shelter by door that opens to outside

Sheltering Dangerously
- Leaving doors, windows open
- Sheltering in an inner room
- Exiting while flames are close

Evacuating Safety
- Pre-test your destination route
- Leave before embers start to fall
- Leave only for somewhere safer

Car Safety
- Cars protect well from grassfire
- Cars may protect from mild fire
- Cars won't protect from forest fire

Township Danger Awareness
- Increased by poorly prepared perimeter
- House-to-house embers increase losses
- Vacated houses more easily destroyed

Township Safety Preparations
- Ex-town: reduce flammable undergrowth
- In-town: increase fire resistant plants
- Monitor public and private planting

Pet Safety Preparations
- Take to safety before risk days
- Update identity tags; photograph pets
- Make pure wool coats and covers

Pet Safety During Threat
- Keep in the house with you
- Leashes and cages kept handy
- Water, food in sturdy bowls

Stock Safety Preparations
- Stock refuges; sprinklers for stables
- Windbreaks and firebreaks
- Photograph valued stock, label photos

Introduction

This updating of *Essential Bushfire Safety Tips* was prompted by the need to clear a way through the media-led mass of conflicting fears and non-facts spread since Victoria's Black Saturday bushfires on 7 February 2009.

This knee-jerk reaction set panic coursing through many communities. It fuelled the oppressive assertion that even well-prepared home defenders were likely to die; brought calls to prohibit defending homes; urged that every country town be mandatorily evacuated; and asserted that the only way to ensure safety is to abandon your home to its fate. It has undone 20 years of effective understanding of bushfire safety.

Assumptions were made. People died defending their homes, therefore defending means death. People died 'staying', therefore staying means death.

When there has been a drowning, we ask, 'Did they swim outside the flags?' When there has been a road accident, we ask, 'Were they speeding?' When there has been a house fire, we ask, 'Did they have a smoke alarm?' It is a sickening anomaly that more people were killed at or in their houses on Black Saturday than in any other bushfire. But reality checks are needed after bushfire tragedies, too. We need to ask, 'Had those who died defending known thoroughly how to do so?' 'Had those who died sheltering known the rules for safe sheltering?'

The 2009 Royal Commission into the Victorian Bushfires did not ask these questions. Took no evidence on them. Nor did it investigate why so many homes were saved, and how. Left us with no data as to why some home defenders died, while others did not. Not until after it presented its findings, and research by bushfire scientists emerged, were we to know the facts.

Far from affirming a justification for the 'stay and you may die' outcry, the research showed that the vast majority of Black Saturday deaths of those who stayed with their houses were not caused by the fact of staying. That they were caused by staying without having sufficient knowledge, and without having been sufficiently prepared in advance. And that awareness, knowledge, and appropriate reaction could have saved them. The post-Black Saturday findings of bushfire scientists John Handmer, Saffron O'Neil and Damien Killalea AFSM showed that only 5% of those who died at home on Black Saturday were engaged in *any* kind of active defence, and that very few of those who died had a comprehensive fire plan.

It is extremely rare for people who are very well prepared to die defending their homes. It is entirely possible for people who are thoroughly prepared physically, emotionally and knowledgeably, who have reduced the flammable vegetation from around an ember-protected house, to safely defend it on Code Red or any other days.

Bushfire dangers vary greatly. From a few bushfires, home defence could be perilous and early evacuation wise. From most bushfires, however, home defence is practicable and evacuation may be an over-reaction.

The post-2009 policy preference for evacuation has failed to warn that historically, over 100 years, more people have died evacuating than staying, and this is because when circumstances require evacuation, traditionally most people *will not* evacuate early enough.

Every Australian needs to know how to react safely to a bushfire threat. Everyone, no matter where they live or whether their preference is to defend their home or not, needs to know how to evacuate safely and shelter safely from a bushfire. To know what to do through every phase of danger and, step by step, to be prepared, to be planned, to be practised.

Officials instilling the post-2009 fear that under severe bushfire conditions no homes can be saved, that death is almost certain for those who try to defend them, and who urge general evacuation, have not thoroughly thought through the multiple possible scenarios and consequences of this policy preference.

For families to pack up and relocate infants, school children, aged parents and pets many times a summer; for farmers to desert their animals; for traders and businesses to shut up shop; for doctors to abandon patients and for hospitals to outsource their ill is not a workable solution. Not everybody has a car. There are many financially needy, aged and disabled rural residents who normally rely on others for transport. At a time of evacuation, they may not be able to depend on this. The usual 'lift' may plan to stay and defend their home. If they evacuate, piled high as it will be with their own family, pets and possessions, there may not be room in their car for an extra person.

Much more is now known about the destruction of houses within townships during a bushfire. Media claims of bushfires 'sweeping through' townships, completely destroying them, are inaccurate and made in ignorance. The actuality is that outer houses can be ignited by flames, firebrands or embers from the burning bush. Houses more than a few streets away can then be ignited by embers blown from these, from the flames of closely adjacent burning houses or from flammable vegetation within the town. This domino effect happens more readily in towns whose residents have evacuated or who do not know what to do. Based on the latest findings of bushfire scientists, this updated edition of *Essential Bushfire Safety Tips* contains a new chapter (Chapter 15) on township protection.

Black Saturday research confirms the findings of every previous post-bushfire investigation. That almost every loss is caused not by 'catastrophic' weather, nor lack of official warning nor by divine displeasure. Nor by 'staying' or 'going'. But by apathy, ignorance and confused understanding.

The hope-destroying position promoted by some bushfire authorities that 'If you live in a high-risk bushfire area, your home will not be defendable on a "Code Red" day' is absolutely incorrect. It is demonstrably untrue. Many, many householders who understood how to react safely to a bushfire threat and who had thoroughly worked out and frequently practised plans, did save their homes, their precious possessions and their families together on that exceptional day. As they have in the past, time and again. Many have written to me saying that it was the knowledge obtained from my books that enabled them to do so.

Sadly, on days of heart-rending decision-making, many families are persuaded that, 'It doesn't matter about the house.' But it matters afterwards.

Afterwards, when they stand in front of the pile of rubble that was once the essence of their life. It is not just a matter of the houses. It is all the precious possessions contained within them. And often the destroyed house itself cannot be replaced, because of insurance clauses or changes in town planning regulations. It matters when the days and years drag on and on in what the family expected to be temporary emergency housing. Their suffering in this situation is relentless: health is affected, marriages broken and sources of income lost.

The anguish and anger is not limited to those whose houses burn: an unpublicised fact is that following the 2009 fires, the official homeless waiting-list was altered to give accommodation preference to the bushfire-homeless over the already-homeless who had been waiting for years in distressed circumstances. To urge the abandonment of homes may be good for the building industry but it is not good for families, the community or the economy. Governments and bushfire authorities should be doing all they can to conserve, not deplete, the state's already critically low housing stock.

Authorities have been unable to cope with post-Black Saturday rebuilding needs. The only way to counteract this trend is for people to know how to make themselves, their bush-surrounded towns and their homes safer from bushfires.

The purpose of *Essential Bushfire Safety Tips* is to enable and empower this process.

Joan K. Webster OAM 2012

1

Understanding bushfire

Bushfire may seem to be the ultimate uncontrollable element.
But it actually behaves in predictable ways.
Burning bush does not have to mean burning houses.

To understand bushfire safety, you need to understand bushfire behaviour.

Ingredients needed for bushfires

Any fire needs		*For a bushfire these are*
• fuel	➡	vegetation
• heat	➡	ignition source, e.g. lightning, arson, spark
• oxygen	➡	wind
• dryness	➡	dry air

Ingredients that increase bushfire danger

1	vegetation	plenty of closely growing dry plants
2	air temperature	above 30°C
3	wind	over 20 km/h
4	dry air	less than 30% relative humidity
5	atmosphere	unstable
6	terrain features	slopes, ruggedness
7	building features	complexity, ceiling spaces, exposed windows, raised floor

Items 2–5 are grouped as } weather

A change in any ingredient can increase or lessen bushfire danger.
We cannot change the weather,
but we can modify vegetation, building features and terrain and
so modify the amount of danger.

1 Vegetation

(See Chapter 8, A protective garden; Chapter 15, Township protection; Chapter 16, Protective chores)
- Bushfires cannot happen without vegetation to burn.
  - ➤ The main fuel contributing to a bushfire is dead and dying vegetation.
  - ➤ Only when this burns and releases enough heat does live vegetation burn.
- The more dense the vegetation, the more intensely and dangerously it burns.
- The more widely spaced the vegetation, the less danger to homes if it burns.
- The closer the vegetation is to houses, the more danger they are in.
- Different types of vegetation ignite, burn, and throw embers differently.
  - ➤ Height of flames, ember output and windblown-reach vary with species.

How vegetation burns

- Grass and shrubs (fine fuel) ignite easily and burn fast and hot.
  - ➤ This heat can kill. But flames subside quickly.
- Tree trunks catch fire more slowly than shrubs.
  - ➤ But their flames last longer.
- Tree leaves ignite more quickly than branches and trunks.
  - ➤ And their flames die down more quickly.
- Trees with rough bark ignite more easily than those with smooth bark.
  - ➤ Loose, burning bark can fly kilometres to spread spot fires.
- A tree can't ignite unless lit from something burning at its base.
- Forests and gardens with dense undergrowth and litter burn hottest and longest.
  - ➤ When fuel density is reduced, the heat and persistence of a fire is reduced.
- Grass fires move fastest.
- Fire that runs along tree tops (crowns) creates a great deal of radiant heat.
  - ➤ But most of this goes up, away from the ground.
  - ➤ Crown fires can't continue unless fed from below by burning fuel.
- Good forest, garden and township management can minimise bushfire danger.
  (See Chapter 8, A protective garden; Chapter 15, Township protection; Chapter 16, Protective chores)

Some fine fuel facts

Increased amount of fine fuel

- Increases the height of the flames.
- Increases the speed with which a fire travels.
- Increases the radiant heat.
- Increases embers and therefore spot fires.

Decreased amount of fine fuel

- Decreases the height of the flames.
- Decreases the speed of the fire.
- Decreases fire intensity and therefore the radiant heat output.
  - ➢ The less radiant heat, the less danger to life.
- Decreases embers.
  - ➢ The less embers, the less danger to houses from spot fires.

**Fuel reduction in your garden
is even more important for the safety of your home and family
than fuel reduction in the bush.**

---

2 Air temperature

- When the air temperature is 30°C or higher, bushfire danger is high.
- When the air temperature is below 20°C, bushfire danger is low. (See *The Complete Bushfire Safety Book*, Chapter 2, Bushfire cycles–Bushfire weather)

3 Wind

The wind direction that can increase bushfire danger varies throughout Australia.

Region	Hot-air firewind	Cool-air firewind
South Australia	North to north-west	South-west
Victoria	North to north-west	South-west
New South Wales	North to north-west	South-west
Tasmania	North to north-west	West
Southern Queensland	North-west to south-west	South-west
Northern Territory	South-east	
Western Australia	East to north-east	

- The hottest winds blow in from the deserts of central Australia.
  - ➤ These are called 'hot-air firewinds'.
- A strong cool-weather change shifts a hot wind to the opposite direction.
  - ➤ These are called 'cool-air firewinds'.
- Wind changes from north-west to south-west can be extremely turbulent and violent.
- A site towards which hot wind generally blows is called the firewind side.
- A site sheltered from wind (as on one side of a hill) is called the lee-side, or 'lee'.
- Wind changes during a bushfire can cause a lee to become a firewind side.
- The most hazardous winds are gusty, caused by a turbulent, unstable atmosphere.
  - ➤ Gusty winds make bushfires hard to control.
- When the wind speed on a hot summer day reaches 35 km/h, be prepared.
- When the average wind speed is below 20 km/h, bushfire danger is low.
- Wind speed is different from fire front speed. (See 'Fire's speed' below)
- Wind direction at any particular place may be different from the prevailing wind. (See *The Complete Bushfire Safety Book*, Bushfire cycles)
- The relationship between wind speed, dry air and dryness of vegetation is complex.

What wind does

- Dries out vegetation, making it more combustible.
- Fans flames.
- Bends flames over so they radiate heat onto unburnt material.
- Blows burning embers and debris ahead to start fresh ignitions.
- Fells trees.
- Lifts inadequately secured roofs off houses.

4 Low relative air humidity (dry air)

- Relative humidity (RH) is the degree of moisture in the air.
- Low RH is the most important factor in creating conditions for dangerous bushfires.
- When the relative humidity of the air is 30% or less, be prepared.
- When the relative humidity of the air is above 60%, bushfire is unlikely.

What low relative humidity does

- Evaporates moisture from vegetation, making ignition easier.
  - ➤ Evaporation from fine fuels (leaf litter, twigs) is very rapid: an hour or so.
  - ➤ It is much slower from larger fuels and building materials: days or weeks.

5 Unstable atmosphere

- Occurs when parcels of heated air rise, mixing disruptively with upper air currents.
  - ➢ When the wind is hot, strong and gusty, be prepared.
  - ➢ Still days with clear blue sky and steady, high air pressure, have low danger.

What unstable atmosphere does

- Draws hot air skywards, brings faster cold air down to the surface.
  - ➢ Flames can rise extremely high.
- Winds at ground level become violently gusty.
  - ➢ Bushfires become hard to manage.
- A towering column of smoke, called a convection column, rises – up to 10 000 m.
  - ➢ This tells you the most dangerous type of bushfire is burning.
- Burning firebrands sucked up into such columns can fly, still alight, 40 km.

6 Terrain features

(See Chapter 6, A protective home site; Chapter 7, A protective property layout)

Slopes

- Fire travelling uphill doubles its speed for each 10° increase in slope.
  - ➢ Up a 20° slope, fire moves four times faster than on flat ground.
- Fire travelling downhill goes proportionately slower.
  - ➢ In intense fires, masses of embers can tumble over from the upslope.
- Flames moving slowly downslope grow very much higher on reaching flat land.
- As flames move up an opposite slope, they grow higher still.

Irregular landforms

- Rugged hills, valleys and the lee of ridges set the air eddying. (See Chapter 6, A protective home site)
  - ➢ These turbulent air currents intensify any bushfire.
  - ➢ Fire whirls, even tornadoes with winds of 250 km/h that can twist trees, can form.

7 Building features

(See Chapter 4, How bushfire destroys houses; Chapter 5, The home as a haven)
- Complex building shapes and cluttered gardens also set the air eddying.

Any change in fuel, weather, land shape or building features

(See Chapters 6, 7, 8 and 9)
- Changes intensity, speed, flame height, radiant heat and ember output.
- Increases or decreases the danger of a bushfire.
- Increases or decreases the manageability of a bushfire.

Bushfire types can range widely:
Slow-moving and manageable on a mild, windless day in light fuels.
Fast-moving and hard to control on a day of hot, dry wind in heavy fuels.

How bushfires behave

The flame front

- A grass fire's flame front burns out at any given spot in less than 1.5 minutes.
- A forest fire's flame front dies down at any given spot in 10–15 minutes.
    - ➢ Depending on amount and type of fuel.

By then:
- ➢ Grass is burnt.
- ➢ Shrubbery and undergrowth are down to a sizzle.
- ➢ Tree trunks burn with disconnected flames.

How fire spreads

- By a chain reaction at the fire front.
    - ➢ The flaming edge heats up neighbouring material.
    - ➢ This dries and ignites.
    - ➢ The fire flares, then dies down as that fuel is consumed.
    - ➢ The flame moves on to fresh fuel.
    - ➢ The part that was first alight smoulders and dies out.
- By sparks and embers thrown from a fire or from burning houses, starting more fires.

Fire's rate of spread depends on

- Type and density of vegetation.
- Air temperature.
- Wind direction.
- Wind speed.
- Relative air humidity.
- Atmospheric conditions.
- The number of new ignitions from sparks and embers.

Fire's speed

- The speed of a flame front (rate of spread) is different from wind speed.
  - ➤ Both are different from the speed in which fire spreads from place to place by embers.
- The fastest known grass fire flame front is 27 km/h.
- The fastest known forest fire flame front is 15 km/h.
  - ➤ Top flame front speed on Black Saturday 2009 was 12 km/h.
  - ➤ Claimed speeds of 100+ km/h are wrong. This relates to momentary flares.
- Mild to average forest fire flame fronts seldom travel more than 5 km/h.

Only the outer houses of towns are usually ignited by the actual bushfire. Inner township houses are generally ignited by other houses.

A flame's life

- In grass fires, 2–5 seconds.
- In forest fires, up to 5 minutes.

The heat of flames

- The life-threatening heat given out by flames is called *radiant heat*.
- The amount of radiant heat from a bushfire is related to its *intensity*.

Radiant heat intensity depends on

- Density of fine fuel (grass, shrubs, litter), which affects size and thickness of flames.
  - ➤ The more dense the fine fuel, the more intense heat is radiated.

How radiant heat behaves

- Wildfires in dense forests radiate at least twice as much energy as grass fires.
- A moving fire radiates up to six times more heat from its head than its back fire.
- At any given spot in a grass fire, radiant heat peaks and falls within 90 seconds.
- At any given spot in a forest fire, radiant heat peaks and falls within 15 minutes.
- Large amounts of radiant heat can kill instantly by heat stroke.
  - ➢ This has happened to unsuitably clothed people trapped by flames.

Fireballs

These happen when
- Flames from rapidly burning fuels sometimes become detached.
  - ➢ They rise quickly and rapidly burn out.

What fireballs can do

- Kill you from heat stroke.
- Drop hazardous sparks and embers.
- Crack windows.

What fireballs can't do

- Cause spontaneous combustion.
- Cause buildings to explode.
- Ignite buildings
- Engulf buildings and destroy them instantly.
  - ➢ They burn out too quickly.

The term *embers* is usually applied to burning material carried on the wind. However, there are two types, and they behave quite differently.

Embers

Ember data

- The term *embers* is commonly used to cover sparks, embers and firebrands.
- **Embers** are generally glowing char, such as may roll from your fireplace.
  - ➢ Wind cannot carry these far, due to the pull of gravity on their rate of travel.
- **Firebrands** are burning strips of bark, especially candlebark and stringybark.
  - ➢ These have aerodynamic properties that enable them to be blown long distances. (See Chapter 8, A protective garden)
  - ➢ In grass fires, the firebrands are generally seed-heads and dung.
- A bushfire's manageability depends on the volume of its embers and firebrands.
- Embers, firebrands and sparks entering houses are the prime cause of destructions. (See Chapter 4, How bushfire destroys houses)
- Embers falling on vegetation cause spot fires that extend bushfire's spread.
- Embers falling on flimsily clothed people cause nasty burns and, at times, death.

Where embers and firebrands fall

- Most thickly within the first 100 m of a fire front.
- Only thinly further than 3 km from a fire front.
  - ➢ Ember amount depends on distance, flame height, vegetation type and density.

How far embers can fly

- 100 m ahead of burning grass.
- 2.5 km ahead of burning pine trees.
- 8 km ahead of a burning eucalypt forest.
  - ➢ Ignitions within towns mostly come from burning outer houses, not the bushfire.
  - ➢ Inner and perimeter township protection can prevent this. (See Chapter 15, Township protection)

How far firebrands can fly

- 10 km ahead of a burning forest.
- 40 km when there is a convection column.

Fire's safer areas

- The back of a fire, where it burns slowest, least intensely and with shortest flames.
    - ➤ Preferably, as far away as possible.

Fire's most unsafe areas

- Immediately downwind of a flame front.
    - ➤ This is where it burns fastest, most intensely and with the tallest flames.
- A flank (side) is the next most dangerous part to be near.
    - ➤ Flanks move slowly.
    - ➤ But a wind change can suddenly turn a quiet flank into a front.

(See Chapter 19, Evacuate, defend or shelter?)

To live safely in a fireprone area you have three options

- Thoroughly prepare your property's defence and your ability to safely defend it.
- Thoroughly prepare your property's security and your ability to safely evacuate.
- Thoroughly prepare your property's security and your knowledge of safe sheltering.
    - ➤ Anyone unable to adhere to one of these should consider moving to a large town.

**Knowledge of bushfire behaviour should be as familiar as a hot dry wind.
You can use this knowledge to protect your property and your life.**

2
The killer factors

People who die in bushfires are seldom killed by contact with flames.
They die metres away because they wear shorts and thongs and summer dresses,
because their heads are uncovered and their lungs unscreened.

Death during bushfires is caused by

1 Radiant heat.
2 Asphyxiation.
3 Dehydration.

1 Radiant heat

- Spreads out, as from a radiator, in a straight line from the heat source.
- Can burn, disable and kill.
- Exposure to excessive radiant heat can cause your body temperature to surge.
- If raised above 40.5°C, your brain's heat-regulating mechanism cannot adjust.
  - ➢ Thermal stress on your body then causes failure of vital organs, collapse and death.
- The effect of such thermal stress on your body is called heat stroke.
- The intense heat radiated from some fire front flames can kill within seconds.
- The radiant heat emitted by the flames of a bushfire is hottest at the fire front.

The killer effect of radiant heat

Is increased by

- The height and depth of flames.
- How close you are to flames.
- How long you are near flames.
- The amount of skin exposed.

Is decreased by

- Keeping away from flames.
- Wearing protective clothing.
  - ➢ It is vital to expose skin at wrists or forearms to be aware of radiant heat level.
- Not staying for long near flames.
- Taking shelter behind a solid substance.

2 Asphyxiation, smoke inhalation and toxic fumes

Asphyxiation

Can happen through

- Breathing in the superheated air near a bushfire.
- Breathing in steam from water poured onto flames.

Smoke inhalation

Can happen through

- Breathing in superfine particles of carbon from burnt materials that form smoke.

Toxic fume inhalation

Can happen through

- Breathing in toxic gases hidden in the smoke spreading through a burning house.

Cannot happen through

- A bushfire 'sucking all the oxygen out of the air'.
  - ➢ With fires in the open, as soon as oxygen is consumed more pours in to replace it.

The killer effects of asphyxiation

- Inhaling superheated air causes your throat to swell and compresses your windpipe.
  - ➢ You choke and can die very quickly.
- Inhaling steam can burn your air passages and cause throat tissues to swell.
  - ➢ You can choke or be left with chronic lung problems.

The killer effects of smoke inhalation

- Inhaling smoke impels its particles into small bronchial tubes and clogs the lungs.
    - You may suddenly not be able to breathe, and die
  or
    - irritated airways may lead to pneumonia or chronic lung inflammations.

The killer effects of toxic fume inhalation

- Inhaling toxic fumes can kill very quickly.
- The most common toxic gas inhaled during bushfire is hydrogen cyanide.
    - It is emitted from smouldering synthetic furnishings, textiles, dyes and plastics.
    - It has a typical smell – like bitter almonds.
    - It can kill a person within seconds of breathing it in.
    - It is only dangerous in enclosed spaces and dissipates in the open air.
- Survivors of serious cyanide gas poisoning may develop heart and brain damage.

The risk of asphyxiation and smoke inhalation

Is increased by

- House contents that give off poisonous gases when ignited.
- Not wearing nose cover when exposed to smoke.

Is decreased by

- Furbishing your home with low-flammability, non-gas-producing materials.
- Covering your nose with wetted cloth or a smoke-filtering mask.
    - Dust mist respirators that filter 0.01 of a micron give good smoke protection.
    - Gardening masks do not give smoke protection.

3 Dehydration

- Happens when you excrete more fluid than you drink.
    - This stresses your kidneys.
    - You can sweat 2 L of body fluid an hour at a bushfire.

The killer effect of dehydration

Is increased by

- Not drinking frequently, or enough.
- Wearing heavy clothing.
- Being in a hot car.
- Small size, age, frailty.
    - ➢ Never take babies, frail people or small animals in a car in bushfire conditions.

Is decreased by

- Drinking every 10 minutes whether you are thirsty or not.

(See *The Complete Bushfire Safety Book*, Chapter 4, Insight into bushfire tragedy and Chapter 15, After the bushfire, for fuller details)

Injury hazards

Burns

- Superficial skin burns can hurt more than deep burns.
- Deep burns are more likely than surface ones to become infected.
    - ➢ Synthetic clothes can melt, fuse to the skin and cause deep burns.
- Even small burns to the face, hands, feet or genitals usually need hospitalisation.
- Any type of burn covering more than 20% of the body endangers life.

Eyes

- Drying of eyes can cause ulceration.
- Soot in the eyes can cause ulceration and blindness.
- Smoke in drivers' eyes can cause them to crash.

Clothing

(See Chapter 12, Protective equipment, 'Survival kit – protective clothing')

- Synthetics touched by embers melt and fuse to skin, causing deep burns.
- Lightweight fabric can be burnt by sparks.
- Fuzzy weaves encourage flame to run over them and up to your face.
- Flowing, draped or flared clothing lets flames under it to reach skin.
- Tight clothing conducts heat that can burn skin.
- Pullovers with polo or loose necks catch hot ash, which falls inside onto skin.

- Heavy clothing can tire you quickly and lead to heat stress.
- Rubber soles can melt and burn.
- Hot hobnails on shoe soles can brand your foot.
- Trouser legs worn inside gumboots let embers fall inside the boot.
  - ➢ To prevent this, wear trouser legs *outside* gumboots and tie them firmly in place.
- Thongs give no protection and may melt.
- Wear gloves only for handling hot materials.
  - ➢ Covered hands can't feel rising heat levels that warn you to take shelter.
  - ➢ Don't rely on a hot face for warning, it can indicate imminent heat stroke.

People cannot endure more than a few kilowatts of radiant heat reaching bare skin. If the skin is completely protected from radiant heat and evaporation of sweat allowed, a fit person can tolerate higher levels of heat.

3
The survival factors

The basic theory behind all bushfire survival is:
Starve the flames of fuel. Shield your body. Protect your airways.
Hydrate your body and your surroundings.

1 Radiant heat

Survival factors are increased by

- Shielding your body.
  - ➤ Best: solid walls, earth, water.
  - ➤ Next best: pure wool clothing.
  - ➤ Excellent: heavy cotton drill clothing.
  - ➤ Very good: layers of clothing, textured fibreglass, aluminium foil covers.
  - ➤ Better than nothing: tree trunks, ruts in roads.
  - ➤ Even turning your body from side to side can help.

2 Asphyxiation, smoke inhalation and toxic fumes

Survival factors are increased by

- Furbishing the house with low-flammability and non-toxic materials.
- A wet cloth tied over your nose.
- Smoke-filtering masks that filter particles 0.01 of a micron diameter (P2 masks).
- Being as low as possible to the floor or ground – smoke and cyanide gas rise.

3 Dehydration

Survival factors are increased by

- Drinking a cup of water or fruit juice every 10 minutes.
  - ➤ Babies need boiled water every 10 minutes.
- Eating juicy fruits.
  - ➤ Their minerals help to keep your blood's electrolyte level balanced.
- Keeping cool, to lessen your body's need to sweat and lose fluid.

Beneficial drinks

- Water.
- Fruit juices.

Hazardous drinks

- Alcohol dehydrates you and clouds your judgement.
- Very cold drinks can cause stomach cramps.

Cooling tips

- Wear protective clothing that is strong and light, rather than heavy. (See below, and Chapter 12, Protective equipment, 'Survival kit – protective clothing')
- Drape a wet towel or gel necktie cooler around your neck.
- Drape a damp cotton net over a cot or invalid's bed to cool the air by evaporation.

Eyes – *protection is increased by*

- Wearing heat-resistant, vented goggles.
- Instilling artificial teardrops or gel frequently.
  - ➤ These can be bought cheaply from chemists and optometrists without prescription.

Clothing – *protection is increased by*

- Loose-fitting, cover-all clothes of heavy-duty cotton.
- Loose-fitting, cover-all clothes of light cotton treated with flame retardant.
- Tight-weave, straight-cut (but not tight) trouser legs tied *over* boots.
- Firmly secured, wide-brimmed, strong cotton hat.
- Strong boots with thick nitrone rubber soles.

The pure wool blanket

- Sparks and embers which fall onto heavy duty pure wool extinguish themselves.
- Smoky air can be filtered by a pure wool blanket wetted over the nose.
  - ➤ There is no need to wet the whole blanket.
- The basic blanket can be built into a full bushfire survival kit. (See Chapter 12, Protective equipment, 'Survival kit')

Many people have survived the most terrible conflagrations with only a heavyweight pure wool blanket and water to drink.

4

How bushfire destroys houses

Look carefully at the scenes of houses destroyed in bushfire.
Around many reduced to rubble, the surrounding trees and garden are untouched.
It is not a bushfire's unstoppable sweeping flames that causes this destruction.
It is the houses' own burning contents, ignited by invading embers.

There are three core vulnerable areas of a house

- Ceiling space.
- Windows.
- Subfloor.

Building damage is caused by

- Fire.
- Wind.

Bushfire ignites buildings with

1 Flying sparks, embers, firebrands and burning debris (most commonly).
2 Direct flames.
3 Radiant heat (rarely).

1 Sparks, embers and burning debris

Can

- Get inside the ceiling space.
    - ➤ Ignite rafters and highly flammable dust.
    - ➤ Develop quickly if the space contains stored goods, birds' nests, or is very dusty.
    - ➤ Build up heat until flammable gases are produced that lift off the roof.
    - ➤ The ceiling collapses and whole house flares up in flames.
    - ➤ Smoulder slowly on rafters if the space is clean, and take hours to become volatile.
- Blow through broken windows and under doors.
    - ➤ Ignite curtains that send flames quickly to the ceiling.
    - ➤ Land on and ignite carpets, furniture, bedding, papers.
    - ➤ Flames then move through clothes cupboards, plastics, kitchen, laundry.
- Lodge in cracks in timber walls.
- Infiltrate through vents.
    - ➤ Smoulder until a flame from them flares up the wall cavity.
- Blow under the house.
    - ➤ Burn dry grass or stored goods, spread fire to floorboards and frame.
- Land on and ignite doormats, sending sparks under the door.
- Land in and ignite fibrous hanging baskets, sending flames to the eaves.
- Lodge in rough gaps between deck timbers.
- Catch in creepers on walls and pergolas, endangering the timber beneath them.

**Embers, showering in their hundreds of thousands each moment,
are whirled many metres ahead of flames.
Firebrands (ribbon bark) can comfortably fly 10 km and have been registered at 40 km.**

---

2 Direct flames

Can

- Ignite walls when vegetation grows, or burning debris piles up, against them.

Can't

- Ignite cladding unless they are spread from something burning against it.
    - ➤ It is hard for an extending flame tip to ignite a solid vertical surface.

3 Radiant heat

Can

- Crack windows and allow embers to blow inside.
- Directly ignite house timbers if it comes from a nearby burning building or dense forest.
- Indirectly dry out timber cladding to allow ignition from adjacent plants.
    - ➢ This rarely happens.

Can't

- Cause houses to ignite spontaneously.
- Cause houses to explode ahead of a fire front.
    - ➢ Mass internal fires started by embers cause the violent disintegration of houses.
- Of its own, ignite the walls of a solid house.

Wind

Can

- Carry sparks, embers and burning debris inside buildings.
- Keep alight sparks caught in the timbers of buildings so that they eventually burn.
- Break windows with hurtling debris.
- Fell trees onto roofs.
- Lift roofs and blow them off.
    - ➢ Masses of firebrands then pour into the house.

Houses burn from the inside outwards, reaching frame and cladding last. The burnt-out shells of brick houses make this plain to see.

Most house ignitions occur when

- Sparks or embers get into the ceiling space.
    - ➢ Through roofing gaps.
    - ➢ Under loose tiles or galvanised sheets.
    - ➢ From eaves ignited by burning leaves in roof gutters.
- Embers enter rooms.
    - ➢ Through windows cracked by radiant heat.
    - ➢ Through windows cracked by direct flame contact from nearby burning plants.
    - ➢ Through windows cracked by build-up of ash or embers on the ledge.
    - ➢ Through windows broken by hurtling debris.

- Sparks slip under doors.
- Burning debris rolls into a subfloor space or against flammable walls.
- Shrubs grown against verandah posts or subfloor gap-boards burn.
- Embers or smouldering rubbish ignite doormats.
- Embers ignite fibrous hanging baskets and send flames to eaves.
- Embers are caught in rough timber decks, cracks in cladding, or creepers on walls.

> **When an ember blown from a bushfire gets inside a house,
> the process is the same as when an unattended ember rolls from the hearth
> or a burning cigarette butt gets lodged in an armchair.
> If the ember is doused, it goes out; if not, the same total destruction results.**

The destruction of a house can develop

- *Slowly* from a small ignition moving through low-flammability contents.
- *Quickly* from a small ignition moving through high-flammability contents.

  In both these situations
  - ➢ Vegetation outside will probably be burnt out before shelterers are forced out.
  - ➢ Survival chances can be lessened by housing density or neighbour's vegetation.
  - ➢ Survival can be helped by protective clothing and your ability to contain ignitions.

- *Violently* from mass ignitions as embers rain in through broken windows or a lifted roof.

  In this situation
  - ➢ Shelterers inside are usually forced out before vegetation outside is burnt out.
  - ➢ Survival is in doubt. Survival chances can be increased by:
    - – wearing protective clothing and sheltering from radiant heat.
    - – having a fuel-free path on which to safely move away from the house.
    - – having carried out good garden vegetation management. (See Chapter 8, A protective garden)

The internally developing fire

- Gathers energy as it moves through house contents, furniture, clothes, equipment.
- Can give off toxic gases from burning items.
- Creeps through a house if it is well sealed and internal doors are closed.
  - ➢ In this case it can take hours to burn a house down.

- Rushes through house and contents if draughts fan the flames.

  or
  - ➢ if hazardous cleaning and other chemicals explode

  or
  - ➢ plastic fittings spread molten fire.
- Can burn in many rooms at once when massive ember entry causes multiple ignitions.
- Can enter many rooms at once when fire is in the ceiling or air conditioner ducts.
  - ➢ In these cases a house can burn down very quickly.
- Internal fire can grow to such pressure it can lift off a roof.
  - ➢ This can *look like* an explosion.
- A spark or ember can't start any of this if someone puts it out.

(See Chapter 21, What to do when bushfire threatens)

What can't happen

- A house can't explode from the heat of an approaching bushfire.
- A house can't ignite spontaneously.
- Flames can't ignite cladding from a distance.
- Radiant heat can't ignite cladding from a distance.
- Fireballs can't ignite a house.

Every burning house sends off its own embers that can ignite more houses.
This can be prevented.

5

The home as a haven

To make your home a haven requires dedication and determination.
It requires thorough preparation, planning, practice – and constant maintenance chores.

There are three core needs of home as haven

- Fuel reduction around house.
- Ember-resistant house structure.
- Householders with thorough bushfire safety knowledge.

The science behind home as haven

- Houses generally ignite from ember penetration.
- Houses burn from the inside outwards.
- Frame and cladding burn last.
  - ➢ This means that if embers can be kept out of the house, you can be safe with it.
- Ember *attack on* the house can be reduced by reducing the vegetation outside it.
- Ember *penetration of* the house can be impeded by improved design and maintenance.
- Buildings take longer to ignite than vegetation.
- Some trees are slower to ignite than others.
- Tree trunks themselves generally burn only in the most intense fires.
- The bark on tree trunks can ignite before the bark on the branches.
- Bark burning on tree trunks can carry fire up to branches and leaves.
- Tree branches take longer to ignite than leaves, grass and shrubs.
  - ➢ This means that a house will not burn simultaneously with nearby vegetation.
  - ➢ Flames and embers take longer to ignite a building than its bordering vegetation.
- As fire moves through vegetation, flames in the vegetation die down.

- You would generally by then be safe outside. (See Chapter 21, What to do when bushfire threatens)
- Wind-blown embers can enter houses before nearby vegetation burns.
- This is why reduction of nearby flammable vegetation is vital. (See Chapter 8, A protective garden)

The survival rate of houses – in even the most extreme bushfires –
is more than doubled when they are defended.
Most that survive have substantially fuel-reduced grounds and ember-blocking features.
Most that are destroyed have dense fuel around them and many ember entry points.

Details of needs

- Protective site features.
- Protective layout of grounds.
- Protective house design features and modifications.
- House well-maintained.
- Fire-minimising furnishings.
- Paths used as fuelbreaks.
- Garden plants spaced and debris cleared.
- Reduction of shrubby vegetation.
- Effective use of low-flammability plants.
- A good reserve water supply. (See Chapter 13, Water for protection)
- Roof sprinkler system if possible.
- Well-prepared and practised people at home who know what to do.

Factors that increase the haven potential of homes

- Block size 5–50 ha.
  - ➢ Enough space for sufficient fuel reduction within your own land.

Factors that decrease the haven potential of homes

- Homes on 0.25 ha blocks or on small blocks in small settlements and villages.
- Neighbours' overgrown vegetation and debris that can threaten your efforts.

Benefits of making your home a haven

- No need to travel during danger to reach an evacuation destination.
- Less likelihood of being made homeless.
- No need to abandon animals.
- You can protect your home and precious possessions.

Hazards of not making your home a haven

- You could be at great risk trying to defend or shelter in a poorly prepared house.
- You could be at great risk trying to find haven elsewhere once bushfire threatens.

Homes and lives are not saved by miracles, but by the well-planned acts of people. The better you prepare your property and your knowledge, the greater the haven. Somewhere else may not necessarily be safer.

6

A protective home site

There is no perfect site where you can feel certain of safety from bushfire.
Equally, there is no site that invites certain destruction.
There are many things you can do to minimise dangers.

Protective sites

- Well down the lee (sheltered) side of a slope or embankment.
  - ➢ Fire moves slowly downhill, allowing more time for home defence.
  - ➢ Ember-laden winds are usually carried up and over ridge, away from the house.
  - ➢ In intense fires, winds tumbling about in the lee of ridges carry masses of embers. (See Chapter 7, A protective property layout, for suggested solutions)
- Flat land.
  - ➢ Less air turbulence. Fire behaviour likely to be more stable and manageable.
  - ➢ Except land at the immediate foot of a slope (see below).

Hazardous sites

- Within 3 km of dense bushland or pine plantation.
  - ➢ Can be reached by firebrands.
- Within 500 m of dense bushland or pine plantation.
  - ➢ Easily bombarded by massive showers of embers.
- On the fringe of outer suburbs or rural towns.
  - ➢ Vulnerable to embers from fires in grass, crop, forest or native parkland.
- Exposed to usual firewind direction.
  - ➢ Embers can arrive early and fast.
- Hilltops or ridges.
- Slopes.
  - ➢ Each 10° rise in angle doubles the speed of fire. (See Chapter 7, A protective property layout, for mitigation strategies)

- The lee side of a hill just below the top.
  - Fire whirlwinds can form here.
- Flat land at the immediate foot of a slope.
  - When fire hits flat land after moving down a slope, flame height quadruples.
- Sites set within flammable vegetation.
- Treeless area within forest.
  - Embers can be sucked into it.
- Very small sites.
  - Not enough room for protectively cleared areas.

Site hazard increases with

- Closeness to dense bushland.
- Closeness to large areas of dry grass or crop.
- Density of flammable vegetation on site.
- Density of housing near bush or grassland.
- Lack of protectively cleared areas or of non-combustible barriers.
- Steepness of slope.
- Proximity to a ridge.
- Ruggedness of landscape.
- Orientation to firewinds.
- Smallness of site.
- Lack of water.

> **Whether the hazards are of site, layout, vegetation or design,**
> **most can be reduced by taking three steps:**
> **define the problems – consider your options – make knowledgeable choices.**

7

A protective property layout

Your property layout can be a fortress against bushfire attack.
High windbreaks can be ramparts to deflect showers of embers.
Wide fuelbreaks can be moats to halt the run of ground-fires.
Terraced landforms can slow flames. Shields can shelter from radiant heat.

A protective property layout can

- Deflect ember-laden winds away from your house.
- Deflect ember-laden winds up and over buildings and so avoid them.
- Lessen the speed and height of approaching flames.
- Limit the probability that a fire will reach your house.
- Stop a bushfire in its tracks.

A hazardous property layout can

- Draw embers to it.
- Pull fire between buildings.

Layout protection features

1 Protective zones of thinned-out vegetation.
2 Windbreaks.
3 Fuelbreaks.
4 Spark screens.
5 Radiant heat shields.
6 Terraced slopes.
7 Removal or safe siting of hazards.

1 Protective zones

Inner zone needs

- Management of an area extending 30–40 m from house.
- Terracing of steep slopes.
  - ➤ Can hinder the reach of flames sweeping up a slope.
- Closely mown grass, irrigated if possible.
- Predominance of European deciduous trees.
- No rough-barked eucalypts.
- No pine trees, even ornamental pencil pines.
  - ➤ Unless pines' lower branches are pruned to 8 m from the ground.
- Loose bark stripped from trees.
- Dead branches removed from trees.
- Dead material removed from tree forks and other plants.
- Nothing flammable grown or stored beneath trees.
- Trees spaced so canopies can't touch.
- Fine-leaved shrubs minimised.
- Predominance of fleshy-leaved plants.
- No flammable mulch.
- No plants grown against windows or walls.
- Wide gravel or concrete paths between garden beds and flammable walls.
  - ➤ To separate the house from vegetation.
- Ground cleared and raked.

Inner zone can protect

- House, sheds, cars, water tanks, woodheaps, machinery, fuels, stock refuge.

Outer zone needs

- Management of an area extending 60 m from house.
- Fine-leaved shrubs and undergrowth well-separated from each other.
  - ➤ By a distance no less than their mature width.
- Loose bark and dead material removed from trees.
- Non-continuous garden beds; that is, plantings in separated clumps.

- Ground litter cleared from beneath trees and around buildings.
  - On open flat land between grass/crops, railway lines, roads, buildings, 10 m.
  - Between *any* bush and buildings, 30–100 m.
  - Between *dense*, high-flammability bush and buildings, 200–300 m.
  - On ridges or very rough ground, 200–300 m.
  - Beyond these distances, undergrowth thinned.
- Terraces cut into very steep slopes.

Outer zone can protect

- House, sheds and vehicles by reducing ember mass blown from burning bushland.
- Garden and orchard from heat scorch of flames.
- Sensitive areas of bushland.

Hot air rising between buildings of varied heights and sizes causes chaotic wind currents. These currents pull flames along behind them, draw sparks and embers into them and skitter burning debris along the ground.

Windbreaks, fuelbreaks, spark screens and heat shields

Minimise

- Wind damage.
- Spark and ember ignitions.
- Flame and radiant heat reach.
- Drying of cladding.
- Cracking of windows.
- Personal danger from radiant heat.
- Stock loss.

Maximise

- Time to deal with spot fires.
- Personal safety and comfort.

2 Windbreaks

- Consist of rows of closely grown tall trees.
- Modify the strength of wind blowing towards protected objects.
- By forcing an approaching wind to rise, can protect an area well beyond it.
- Can protect buildings and stock.
- Conserve soil moisture near them.

Windbreaks can be

- Tall trees or hedges.
- Fences 2 or more metres high.

Windbreaks to protect buildings and stock refuge

- Dense low-flammability hedges such as lilly-pilly or photinia. (See Chapter 8, A protective garden).

Windbreaks to protect crops and grazing stock

- Permeable hedges such as sticky or silver wattle, with smaller plants beneath.

Wind reduction between houses and embankments

- Create a flat area between house and embankment wider than the height of the house.
  - ➤ This can prevent wind from being funnelled behind the house.

Windbreak tips

- Trees with tall bare trunks need bushy shrubs planted in front of them.
- On hilly sites, place windbreaks along ridges.
- The popular cypress may deflect wind efficiently but is highly flammable.

Windbreaks can double as fuelbreaks

- When planted for a length equal to 20–25 times the trees' mature height.
- When trees are set three times their mature height away from any building.
  - ➤ To prevent trees falling on buildings.
- When continued for 100 m beyond buildings.
  - ➤ This reduces wind 'whip-around' that could carry embers to buildings.
- When they surround three sides of buildings.

Wind/fuelbreaks can be

- Low-flammability trees or hedges.
- Non-flammable fences 2 or more metres high.
- Wire-mesh grown over with low-flammability creeper.

Wind/fuelbreaks are most protective when

- Formed of low-flammability, drought-resistant species.
- Planted in three to five close rows, small shrubs front and back graduating to tall trees.
- Tree trunks of each row are staggered to block gaps between other trunks.
  - ➤ This lessens wind turbulence.

Walk round your property and take note of areas that are more windy than others. Block any narrow space that pulls wind through it with a solid gate, fence or plant.

---

3 Fuelbreaks (firebreaks)

- Can stop the run of fire.
- Reduce the radiant heat reaching stock and home defenders.
  - ➤ Work best for grass fires, which don't throw embers as far as forest fires.

Fuelbreaks can be

- Mowed, weed-killed, grazed, gravelled, irrigated, ploughed, burnt or green areas.
  - ➤ Mowed and slashed areas must be raked, and cuttings removed.
- Creeks, roads, golf courses, sports ovals.
- Swimming pools, courtyards, tennis courts.
- Paths between buildings and plants.
- Driveways. Most protective when:
  - ➤ 4 m or more wide.
  - ➤ On flat or only gently sloping land.
- Low-flammability trees such as European deciduous species.
- Low-flammability crops such as green lucerne.
- Vegetable patches.
- Green lawns, or beds of succulents.

Fuelbreaks need to be

- All around the property, not just on the usual fireward side.
  - ➢ Wind direction can change during a bushfire.
- Both sides of paddock fences.
- As far away as possible from trees.
- Of varying widths according to forest density, tree type, crop and ground slope.

Fuelbreaks near bushland need

- On ridges or very rough ground: 200–300 m cleared around buildings.
- Between *dense* forest and buildings: 200–300 m cleared beneath trees.
- Between *any* forest and buildings: 30–100 m cleared.
  - ➢ Beyond 30–100 m: thin undergrowth to a park-like state.
- Open flat land between grass, crops, railway lines, roads or buildings: 10 m cleared.
  - ➢ More for every degree of slope. Terrace very steep slopes.

Fuelbreaks give most protection

- Parallel to the prevailing wind.
  - ➢ This helps to narrow a fire and slow its speed.

Fuelbreak tips

- As firebreaks, they are not unconditionally effective.
- In grass fires, burning seed-heads can send sparks and embers across them.
- In forest fires, embers easily fly across them.

**Low flammability trees, hedges and walls are triple safety features:
wind, spark and radiant heat shields.**

---

4 Spark screens

- Can obstruct, capture and extinguish sparks.
- Can shield a roof or wall from a shower of embers.
- Can prevent sparks entering open or cracked windows.

Spark screens can be

- Metal mesh maximum 1.8 × 1.8 mm.
  - ➢ Gives protection from sparks.
  - ➢ Reduces heat stress by 27%.
- Metal mesh maximum 3 × 3 mm.
  - ➢ Gives protection from firebrands and mild fire.
- Smooth-barked low-flammability trees with spreading large-leafed canopies.
  - ➢ European deciduous species are good examples.
  - ➢ If cleared of dead matter and litter, sparks and embers landing in them can die out. (See Chapter 8, A protective garden)

Mesh spark screens can protect

- Windows and doors.
  - ➢ Installed on the outside, delays cracking from heat and hinders spark entry.
- Subfloor gapboards.
- Area under raised timber decks or 'stilt' houses.
- Vents.
- Air conditioners that have external intakes.
- Chimney openings.
- Gates that have gaps in them.
- Buildings and gardens.
  - ➢ A low mesh fence can hinder the run of a mild grass fire.

Tree spark screens are most protective when

- Spreading over the fireward side of a roof.

Tree spark screen tip

- Tree canopy must not be able to touch roof or walls in a high wind.
  - ➢ Prune 2–3 m away from roof or wall.

5 Radiant heat shields

Protect

- Home defenders from the heat of flames.
- Exit doors.

- Windows.
- Flammable cladding.
- Bushfire shelter entrance.
- Stock refuge area
  - ➤ For a horse, make a heat shield 3–4 m long and at least as tall as the horse.
- Pet accommodation.
- Special areas of garden.

Radiant heat shields can be

- Non-flammable walls 2 or more metres high.
- Low-flammability hedges.
- Earth mounds.

Radiant heat shields need to be

- Constructed of non-flammable material.
- Strong enough to withstand winds over 150 km/h.
- High and wide enough to screen the object of protection.
  - ➤ At least 2 m high and 3 m wide.

Radiant heat shields give best protection

- No more than 10 m from house and outbuildings.
- No more than 5 m from an exit door or special area of protection.
- On the downside of a slope.
- Sited between home defenders and flammable vegetation.
- Sited between water supply outlet and flammable vegetation.

Radiant heat shield tip

- Do not allow flammable vegetation to grow on or near it.

Some property features, though necessary, are hazardous during a bushfire. However, these can be sited, stored or modified to minimise danger.

---

6 Terraced slopes

- Terracing can hinder the rush and long reach of flames sweeping up a steep slope.
- Cut into downslope to make wide areas of flat ground alternating with vertical banks.
  - ➢ The flat area needs to be wider than the height of the house.
  - ➢ Consult a surveyor for advice on ideal balance between flat areas and height of banks.

7 Safe siting of hazards

Timber fences and walls

- Edge with paths of gravel or paving.
- Clear vegetation for at least 2 m from them.

Firewood

- Store 20 m from your house on the lee-side.
- Store in an enclosed shed with a leeward-facing entrance.
  - ➢ Entrance sheltered by a spark-proof screen or door.
  - ➢ Heavy-duty builders' foil, weighted down, can make a useful temporary cover.
- Do not stack under trees, near long grass or against house wall.

Incinerators

- Site 3 m from fences and buildings.

Fuel tanks

- Site 50 m away from buildings, haystacks and other fuel tanks.
- On the lee-side of your house.
- On the downside of a slope.
- Are safest underground.
  - ➢ Underground fuel tanks need permanent sump drainage pumps.
- Fit both above-ground and ground-level fuel tanks with water-sediment drain valves.
- Do not site on concrete.
  - ➢ Leaking fuel could trickle towards a building.
- Tanks on porous ground need to be raised on metal stands.
- Surround stands with an earth wall or ditch.
- Bungs must be kept tight on drums.
  - ➢ Outside refill tins need non-flammable housing with metal mesh over vents.

Power lines

- Are safest underground.
- If above-ground, are safest if run in the direction of the usual firewind.
- Should be no closer to a tree than its full-grown height.
- Should have as short a distance as possible between poles.

Haystacks

- Are safest enclosed in a shed.
    - ➢ Wall in at least on the fireward side.
    - ➢ Leave air space between shed walls and hay to prevent spontaneous combustion.
- Lay out unenclosed stacks singly in separate paddocks.
    - ➢ In fallow paddocks or green summer crops.
    - ➢ In paddocks where stock can graze right up to them.
- Have 4.5 m of bare ploughed ground between each stack.
    - ➢ For 9–12 m beyond the bare ground, vegetation must be mown or grazed.
- Site away from power lines.
- Site near a water supply.

**The more careful attention you pay to all possible protective measures,
the more safety you will provide from bushfire's dangers:
sparks, embers, flame reach, radiant heat and wind.**

8

A protective garden

Vegetation and other fuel in your garden can provide more fuel than that in the bush. Managing garden fuel reduces the danger of embers and flames encroaching from bush. A protective garden creates a lifebelt around your home.

There are three core aspects of a protective garden

- Distance of flammable vegetation from buildings.
- Distance between individual flammable plants.
- Absence of ground litter and clutter.

Protective gardens have

- Sizeable areas of gravel or close-mown grass, well-irrigated if possible.
- Fences of stone, brick, other masonry or metal.
- Trees and shrubs planted singly or in separated clumps.
  - ➢ This prevents plant-to-plant ignition and 'walls of flame'.
  - ➢ Flames will be isolated, radiant heat less and embers more sparse.
- No native or other leaf-shedding trees within 50 m of your house.
  - ➢ Leaf and litter fall on extremely dry, windy days can endanger your house.
- Trees and shrubs as well-irrigated as possible.
- Leaf litter reduced to the equivalent height of very closely mown grass.
- No pine trees, including ornamental pencil pines, within 50 m of your house.
  - ➢ Unless lower branches are pruned to 8 m from the ground.
  - ➢ Pines' naturally low-growing branches increase their chance of ignition.
- Predominance of European deciduous trees.
  - ➢ These drop fewer leaves in summer.
  - ➢ Even on Black Saturday 2009, trees such as oak and ash did not ignite.
- Areas of fleshy plants.
- Other low-flammability plants.

- Dense-canopied low-flammability trees near firewind side of house. These can:
  - Slow the wind to help prevent the roof lifting off.
  - Protect roof and walls by absorbing sparks and small embers.
- Thick-barked trees.
- Smooth-barked trees.
- Dead matter removed from trees and shrubs.
- Tree trunks stripped of loose bark.
  - Burning streamers can fly long distances.
- Plants that revive well after a fire.
- Trees' understoreys cleared of vegetation and debris.
  - Flames can rise two to six times the height of burning matter.
  - A tree can't burn unless it's ignited from something burning at its base.
  - Short grass, if burning, will not ignite a tree canopy.
- Trees pruned 2 m from the ground, 2 m from walls and 2 m from roof.
  - Trees close enough to buildings to need such pruning should be smooth-barked.
- Pine trees' lower branches pruned to 8 m from the ground.
  - Pruning to 6 m did not prevent *Pinus radiata* crowning in the Canberra 2003 fires.
- Beds of low-flammability plants such as succulents and vegetables.
  - Embers will fizzle out in them.
- Safe composts, such as pebbles, granitic sand or road-metal crushings 75 mm deep.
- Wide paths between mulch, plants and flammable walls.
- No shrubs against flammable walls.
- No shrubs against windows.
- Litter raked and removed for 20 m around the house.
  - Add 0.5–1 m for every degree of slope.
- Lawn substitute such as low-flammability groundcover or gravel.
- Non-flammable fences.
- Timber fences edged with gravel or paved paths.
- Open-mesh wire fences grown over with low-flammability creeper.
- Earth mounds or ditches on the firewind sides of buildings.
  - These can catch bowling, burning debris.
- Non-flammable outdoor furniture and door mats.
- Toys, boxes and papers (anything flammable) moved under cover on fire danger days.
- Firewood covered and stacked well away from house and trees.
- Radiant heat shields.
- Perimeter sprinklers
  - With butterfly-spray nozzles to protect garden for 10 m from house.
  - With impact-spray nozzles to penetrate adjacent bush.

- Nearby bushland on fireward sides of the property thinned and fuel reduced. (See Chapter 7, A protective property layout)
  - ➤ Depending on topography, fuel density and type, this can need 30–500 m.
- Nearby bushland fuel reduced and cleared of ground litter.
- Road verge and naturestrip grass closely mown, grazed, gravelled or paved.

Fire can't burn what you've cut back. It can't burn bare earth or gravel paths.
It can't burn trees if there's nothing growing under them.
It can't ignite cladding or crack windows if there's nothing growing near them.

Hazardous gardens have

- Clutter.
- Long dry grass.
- Flammable mulch on garden beds.
  - ➤ Fine chips, straw, bark, sawdust and dung pats can stay alight for 15 minutes.
  - ➤ Embers of heavy woodchips can stay alight for more than 30 minutes.
  - ➤ In the Canberra 2003 fires, masses of mulch embers ignited other gardens and homes.
- Timber fences.
  - ➤ These can act as a fuse, carrying fire from house to house.
- Firewood stacked against the house.
  - ➤ Ignited woodheaps can burn for an hour and produce unsurvivable heat.
- Toys, boxes, papers, tyres, building materials or paint lying about.
  - ➤ Even bicycles can add to the fuel load.
- Flammable outdoor furniture.
- Predominance of flammable trees.
  - ➤ Eucalypts and conifers are notably flammable.
  - ➤ Burning pine needles can be blown 2.5 km, eucalypt leaves 4 km.
- Flammable shrubs that touch each other.
  - ➤ When trees and shrubs touch each other, fire spreads among them.
- Long grass, fine-leafed shrubs, litter and dead leaves.
- Dead plants and dead parts of plants.
- Plants grown against windows.
- Plants grown against flammable walls.
- Plastic pots against flammable walls.
- Shrubs or long grass grown under trees.
- Trees with loose stringy bark.
- Trees with long ribbony bark.
  - ➤ Burning candle or stringy-bark streamers can be blown 8–35 km.

- Rough-barked trees.
- Twiggy trees and shrubs.
- Trees that continually drop leaves in dry weather.
  - ➢ Eucalypts can drop enough leaves on one hot, dry day to fill gutters.
- Trees with ground-sweeping lower branches.
  - ➢ Pines and some wattles are typical.
- Old trees and shrubs.
  - ➢ A hedge may look green but its core can be old, brittle and dry.
- Continuous tree canopies.
  - ➢ Act as a fuse.
- Parallel rows of trees.
  - ➢ Create wind tunnels that can draw embers to your house.
- No trees.
  - ➢ A treeless patch within a forest draws flying embers down into it.
- Creepers growing on pergolas, verandah posts, flammable walls or fences.
  - ➢ Embers lodging in them can ignite the building.
- Trellis against flammable walls.
- PVC sheeting under mulch.
- Treated pine features.
  - ➢ Give off cyanide gas when burning.
- Railway sleepers.
  - ➢ Catch embers.
- Fibrous hanging baskets hung against flammable walls.

Close-growing, flammable plants accelerate fire.
The flames from any fire burning in them emit much radiant heat.
Spaced, low-flammability plants slow down a fire and make it more manageable
– in even the most extreme conditions.

Low-flammability plants

- Some plants are naturally less flammable than others.
- All plants burn differently.
- Different parts of the same plant burn differently.
- Some species just char and if they are not touching other plants cannot not spread fire.
- Other species flare up and will spread flame and throw sparks to start spot fires.
- Supreme among low-flammability plants are European deciduous trees.

Low-flammability plants can

Minimise

- Flame-front spread.
- Radiant heat.
- Showers of sparks and embers.
- Spot fires.
- Building ignitions.

They therefore

- Reduce the amount of flame, embers and radiant heat reaching a building.
- Ease the task of defending homes.
- Provide a safe retreat for home defenders and shelterers.

Maximise

- Time to deal with landing embers.
- Safety and comfort.
- House and personal survival.

Properties of low-flammability plants

- Minerals such as ammonium phosphate and sodium chloride in leaves.
- Low cellulose (fibre) content in leaves.
- Lack of waxes, oils and resin in leaves.
- Broad leaves.
- Thick leaves and twigs.
- Sappy leaves and twigs.
- Smooth bark.
- Non-peeling bark.
- Lowest part of canopy is high above the ground.
- Youth of plant.
- Low leaf or bark drop during the bushfire season.
  - ➤ The bushfire season varies throughout Australia: the further north, the earlier. (See Chapter 19, Protective travelling)

Properties of hazardous plants

- Low mineral content in leaves.
- High fibre content in leaves.
- Waxes, oils and resin in leaves.

- Long thin leaves.
  - ➤ Plants with long thin leaves have adapted to dry air and fire.
- Thin twigs.
- Brittle leaves and twigs.
- Rough bark.
- Peeling bark.
- Bark that is stringy or hairy.
- Capacity to produce burning brands.
- Capacity to spit sparks.
- Dead leaves and twigs on plant.
- Dead material in the canopy.
- Production of leaf or bark drop during the bushfire season.
- Lowest part of the canopy close to the ground.
- Aged plant.

Be aware that

- Even low-hazard plants can dry out in drought and so become flammable.
- Even highly flammable plants may not burn if kept well hydrated.
  - ➤ Eucalypts along Marysville's small creek did not burn on Black Saturday.
- Few plants are fully fire-proof, but ignition rates definitely vary from reluctant to rapid.
(See *The Complete Bushfire Safety Book* for an extensive list of low-flammability plants)

A flammability rating test

- Take a small bunch of leaves to an incinerator or gas stove.
  - ➤ Have a bucket of water into which to drop burning leaves.
- Slowly move leaves towards the flame.
- Those that are hard to light or merely splutter are low-flammability.
- Those that catch fire far from flame, flare quickly or spit are highly flammable.
- Try the same test with dead samples of the same plants.

**By reducing fine fuel and surface litter
you can reduce the intensity of an approaching bushfire from very high, to low.
Where vegetation has been cleared or thinned,
fire moves away to more plentiful fuel.**

9

A protective house design

> We cannot stop bushfires from happening.
> But there are many ways we can stop them from getting into our buildings.
> We can modify and adapt buildings to minimise damage.

A bushfire-resistant house design

- Has simple exterior lines.
  - ➢ Attachments and additions provide angled junctions that trap embers and debris.
- Has one wing only to avoid ember-trapping return corners.
  - ➢ Improve the safety of unavoidable return corners with non-combustible materials.
- Has a strong roof.
- Has a simple roof shape.
  - ➢ Avoids ember-trapping hips and hollows.
- Has gaps sealed from spark and ember entry.
- Has vulnerable areas screened from radiated heat.

Areas needing special protection

- Ceiling space.
- Windows.
- Subfloor.
- Vents and crevices.

Bushfire-resistant house design on slopes

- House snuggled into slope to shelter from fire-laden winds.
  - ➢ Flat areas wider than house height between it and approaching upslope.

Important protective features

- Shutters.
- Metal mesh.
- Gap filler.
- Insulation.
- Sprinklers.

Shutters

- Completely protect windows and doors.
- Can be commercially manufactured or personally improvised.
- Can be permanent or temporary.

Metal mesh flywire – maximum 1.8 x 1.8 mm

- Hinders spark entry.
- Reduces heat stress by 27%.
- Delays cracking of glass by radiant heat during a mild fire.
- Is cheap, efficient and easy to install.

Use metal flywire

- To surround raised subfloor spaces.
- On the outside of windows.
- Over gaps.
- To cover vents.
- To cover chimneys.
- To cover skylights and ventilation whirligigs.
- To cover air-intake components of air conditioners.
- Around property fence-lines to hinder grass fires.
- Over polycarbonate or vine-covered pergolas.

Gap filler

- Prevents spark and ember entry through cracks and joins.
- Can be fire-rated and expandable.

Insulation

- Will hinder, and can prevent, ignition by embers or flames.
- Most useful to protect from embers in ceiling space or flames under floor joists.

Sprinklers

Can completely protect house from embers and flames.

A house that will resist ember attack does not need to be complicated.
A single storey with no ceiling space, strong roof, slab floor and protected windows
will generally be defendable and a safe refuge.

Building a bushfire-resistant house

Foundations – protective

- Concrete slab.
  - ➤ No subfloor space.
- Raised subfloor enclosed with non-flammable surround.
  - ➤ Brick, stone, fibre-cement, fine metal mesh.
- Stumps of brick, concrete or stone.

Foundations – hazardous

- Raised with no protective surround.
- Unprotected timber stumps.

Subfloor or subdeck surrounds – protective

- Timber gap-board surround closed in for 1 m from ground level.
- Subdeck area free of vegetation, preferably completely closed in.
  - ➤ Use any non-flammable material, or metal mesh.
  - ➤ Seal well at the top.
- Vents covered with metal flywire.

Subfloor or raised deck – hazardous

- Completely open subfloor.
    - ➤ Tumbling, burning debris has unhindered access to floor and wall cavity.
- Uncovered timber gap-boards.
    - ➤ Embers can blow through to stumps, joists, floorboards, wall cavity and frame.
    - ➤ Rough boards can catch sparks.
- Uncovered vents.
    - ➤ Sparks can get through to lodge in the angle of stumps and floor joists.
- Flammable surround at ground level.
    - ➤ Burning debris or ash piled against it can ignite even sturdy timbers.
- Uninsulated metal supports.
    - ➤ Can collapse if exposed to sustained high heat.

**An ignition under the floor is hard to get at and douse.
Prevention can be relatively easy.**

Floors – protective

- Underside of timber floors sealed with continuous insulation.
    - ➤ Fibreglass-based batts, aluminium foil laminate, plasterboard or fibre-cement.
- Electric wiring, gas and water laid through floor instead of through cavity walls.
    - ➤ No construction gaps in walls for sparks to slip through.

Floors – hazardous

- Exposed timber underside.

Exterior wall design – protective

- As few nooks and corners as possible.
    - ➤ Burning debris won't be trapped so easily against the house.
    - ➤ Fewer wind eddies.
- More than one exit door.
    - ➤ At least one exit door opening onto leeward, sheltered space.
    - ➤ This exit door protected with radiant heat shield.

- Wide verandah with non-flammable floor and metal posts.
  - ➢ Helps protect windows.
  - ➢ Less radiant heat reaches walls.

Exterior wall design – hazardous

- Multiple wings.
  - ➢ Create corners that trap burning debris.
  - ➢ Hard for defenders to monitor all areas.
- Multiple storeys.
  - ➢ Stairwell can act as flue to draw fire to next floor.
  - ➢ Defenders or shelterers could become trapped upstairs.

Interior wall design – protective

- Exit doors easily reached from any part of house.
- Minimum walls in an open-plan design.
  - ➢ Large areas inside the house can be monitored for embers at the one time.
  - ➢ Ember entry can be controlled and internal spot fires doused easier.
- Maximum inner walls with door-enclosed rooms.
  - ➢ Rooms can be shut off to hinder flame spread from ignitions.

Interior wall design – hazardous

- Numerous passages, angles or dead ends.
  - ➢ Shelterers seeking an exit easily become confused in smoke.

Internal wall linings – protective

- Brick, stone, tiles and plasterboard.

Internal linings – hazardous

- Some decorative materials.
  - ➢ Give off toxic gas when heated.

Bench tops and storage cupboards – protective

- Solid untreated timber.
- Marble, granite.
- Metal, concrete.

Bench tops and storage units – hazardous

- Laminate.
  - ➢ Burning molten ribbons spread fire through room.

Wall frame – protective

- Timber and metal frames insulated on inner and outer surfaces.
  - ➢ Inner insulation hinders spread of fire to interior from wall cavity.

Wall frame – hazardous

- Timber frames can be ignited from a subfloor fire rising through wall cavity.
- Metal frame won't ignite but can warp from the intense heat of burning contents.

Wall cavities – protective

- Packed with fibreglass or mineral-wool batts.

Insulation

- Install under roof ridges, between roofing sheets and under eaves.
- In ceiling space, above and below, between rafters.
- In cathedral ceilings between lining and roof.
- Beneath timber floors.
- In wall cavities.
- Around the first metre of posts supporting timber verandah, carport or deck.
- In garage walls and doors.
- Between window shutters and glass.
- In refuge room or bunker walls, doors, floor and ceiling.

Insulation – protective

- Fibreglass, mineral wool and aluminium foil laminates.
  - ➢ These will not ignite, spread flame, build up heat or develop smoke.

Insulation – hazardous

- Tarpaper.
  - ➢ Highly flammable.
- Loose-fill materials.
  - ➢ Can entrap sparks between pieces.
- Bituminous impregnated foam (black jack) and neoprene caulking.
  - ➢ Unstable in heat.
- Polystyrene and polyurethane.
  - ➢ Slow to ignite, but once alight give off toxic gas.

A stone or brick home is not safer than a timber home.
Look at all the empty shells of burnt-out brick and stone buildings.

Wall cladding data

- Masonry cladding will not protect from ember entry.
  - ➢ Brick, concrete and stone buildings are routinely destroyed by bushfires.
- Masonry cladding will not ignite from direct flame.
- Well-maintained timber cladding does not easily ignite from direct flame.
  - ➢ Contrary to media myth, timber houses routinely survive the worst bushfires.

Timber – protective

- Boards sanded smooth and well-painted.
- Logs of sturdy, fire-resistant timber.
- Gaps filled with fire-rated, expandable sealant.
- Base surrounded with non-flammable covering for 1 m up from ground level.
- Nothing growing against it.

Mud brick – protective

- External load-bearing pillars encased in non-flammable material.

Fibre-cement – protective

- Sheets 9 mm thick.
  - ➤ This protects only from mild bushfire.
  - ➤ Can crack and break up under intense radiant heat and expose frame.

Cladding – hazardous

- Plastic or vinyl.
  - ➤ Distorts under heat to expose wall cavities.
  - ➤ Embers can lodge in cracks at joins.
- Oiled or rough-sawn board, wooden shingles.
  - ➤ Embers can catch in their splits, cracks and edges.
- Pine logs that are treated with copper-chrome-arsenate salts.
  - ➤ Flames run up them.
  - ➤ Smoke from these is toxic.
- Metal sheeting.
  - ➤ Conducts heat and can warp.
  - ➤ Tests that show steel cladding survives flame have ignored ember dangers.

Paint – protective

- Normal house paint well-maintained over a smoothly sanded surface.
  - ➤ Paint marketed as fire-retardant has not yet been proved effective.

Paint – hazardous

- Oil and varnish are highly flammable.

Windows – protective

- Covered with permanently fitted roll-down metal shutters.
- Covered with attachable emergency shutters. (See 'Temporary shutters', below)
  - ➤ Will prevent glass being smashed by debris hurled by violent winds.
- Covered with fine metal mesh on the outside of glass.
  - ➤ Will prevent cracking by radiant heat.
- Sloped sills in all circumstances – best of brick.

Windows – hazardous

- Unprotected glass.
- Thin glass.
- Badly-fitted sashes.
- Sealant of putty.
  - ➤ Putty, once set, will not flex, so that expanding hot glass is forced out and cracks.
- Flat sills.
- Oiled, rough-sawn or badly painted timber sills.
- Unprotected skylights.
- Windows with adjacent plants.

Window glass – protective

In areas of high fire intensity or strong wind hazard

- Shutters installed on firewind sides.
  - ➤ To stop windblown debris causing breaks that let in embers.
- Double-glazed or toughened glass.
  - ➤ Glass 8 mm thick withstood the Black Saturday fire at Steele's Creek.
- Wire-mesh reinforced glass.
- Silicone sealant.
  - ➤ Silicone allows glass to expand and stay intact if cracked by radiant heat.
- Criss-crossed with adhesive tape, glass can stay intact if cracked by radiant heat.

In areas of milder hazard

- Full-length flyscreens of metal mesh on the outside.

Window frames – timber

- Can ignite.
  - ➤ Less likely to ignite if smooth, sloped, well-painted, dense hardwood.

Window frames – metal

- Cannot ignite.
  - ➤ Can warp once a house is burning.

Window sills – protective

- Brick or other masonry.
- Well-painted timber.
- Well-sloped.
  - ➢ Burning debris can slide off.

Window sills – hazardous

- Poorly painted timber.
  - ➢ Can catch sparks and burning debris.
- Flat.
  - ➢ Ash and embers can build up on them, crack glass or ignite frame.

Window sashes

- Protect with draught excluders.

Window shutters

(See *The Complete Bushfire Safety Book*, Chapter 8, Design to keep bushfire out of buildings)

- Can protect windows, doors, balconies and verandahs.
  - ➢ Window protection is no substitute for fuel reduction around the house.

Best protection

- Non-flammable.
- Cover both window and frame.
- Fit snugly, parallel to the glass.

Shutters – permanent

Best protection

- Roll-down metal blinds, close-fitting.
  - ➢ Stop the full force of hurtling debris.
  - ➢ Prevent windows from breaking.
  - ➢ Prevent embers from landing on ledge.
  - ➢ Prevent spark entry.
- Must have manual (preferably internal) operation in case electricity fails.

Useful protection

- Roll-down metal blinds, angled.
  - ➢ Can stop the full force of hurtling debris, but allow embers to land on ledge.
- Slatted shutters.
  - ➢ Slats must be angled out and down and fully covered with metal mesh.

For even greater protection on any type

- Fix insulation batts or heavy duty foil on the inside of shutters.

Shutters – temporary

- Fibreglass/mineral-wool batts sandwiched between non-flammable sheets.
  - ➢ Such as 9 mm plasterboard, 19 mm hardboard, fibre-cement or corrugated iron.
- Insulation batts or foil sandwiched between two sheets of light welded steel mesh.
  - ➢ Foil protects from radiant heat.
  - ➢ Mesh protects from mild impact.
- Heavy-duty foil attached with hooks or velcro.
  - ➢ Can be made into a roller-blind.
- Heavy-duty foil under chicken wire, attached by screws or hooks.
  - ➢ Each of the above will withstand a short burst of high fire-front heat.
  - ➢ These are good alternatives for people who rent.

Shutters – hazardous

- Roll-down, angled shutters can allow embers to land on window ledge.
- Slatted shutters can catch and retain embers if not closely fitted and well-sloped.
- Velcro strips can soon become brittle when exposed to weather.
- Roll-down flat shutters with no manual operation.

Skylights

- Burning embers can fall straight through them.
- Plastic skylights can melt.
  - ➢ A flue effect occurs: internal ignitions accelerate; flames are drawn skywards.
- Commercial 'insulating shields' will not protect from a shower of embers.
  - ➢ Protect with closely fitted metal mesh covers.
  - ➢ Protective glass-diffusers, installed at ceiling level, are available.

Air conditioners – roof-mounted evaporative models

- Allow spark entry.
- Components of units can ignite during bushfire.
- Burning beads of plastic can be conducted through vents into rooms below.
- Burning beads of plastic then pour into rooms below vents.
- Conduits channel fumes throughout the house.
  - ➤ Cover unit air-intake with fine metal mesh.
  - ➤ Cover internal vents with heavy-duty foil.

Exterior doors – protective

- Solid core construction.
  - ➤ A door like this will take 30 minutes to burn through.
- Full-length, strong metal mesh flywire door on outside.
- On public buildings, install roll-down metal shutters.
- Strong latches and self-closers.
- Non-combustible draught excluders at base.
- Non-combustible draught stripping all round.
- Removable non-flammable covers for pet doors or letterbox slots.
- Hinged covers for keyholes.
  - ➤ Or plug with soap or mouldable mastic.

Flywire doors – protective

- Metal frames.
- Mesh maximum 1.8 × 1.8 mm.
- Bronze mesh on bronze frames.
- Stainless steel mesh on stainless steel frames.
- Aluminium mesh on aluminium frames.

Flywire doors – hazardous

- Timber frames with crosspieces.
  - ➤ Can catch embers.
- Fibreglass mesh.

Interior doors – protective

- Solid core, 30-minute fire-rated.
- Draught-proofed.

Ceilings – protective

Vital for protection

- Ceiling space inspection trapdoor.
- Ceiling space cleared of dust and all flammable items and materials.

Best protection

- No ceiling space (cathedral ceiling), insulated between its roofing layers.
  - ➤ No enclosed space in which smouldering can build up to explosive flashover.

Good protection

- Rafters insulated above and below.
  - ➤ Two layers of aluminium foil, with fibreglass or mineral wool between.
- Ceiling of low-flammability material that doesn't emit toxic fumes if smouldering.
- Ceiling material reinforced to hinder collapse if rafters ignite.
- Gaps on all outer surfaces sealed.
  - ➤ Spots of light seen from inside a ceiling space show where sparks could enter.
- Ceiling space easily accessible from inside the house.
- Facilities to check for and douse sparks and embers entering ceiling space.

Ceiling space – hazardous

- Any roof/ceiling space. (See Chapter 16, Protective chores)
  - ➤ Sparks and embers can enter unnoticed.
  - ➤ Ignition can take hold, unseen by defenders or shelterers.
  - ➤ Heat can build up until flammable gases lift off the roof.
  - ➤ The ceiling collapses and whole house flares up in flames.
- Ceiling space used to store goods, papers or rubbish.
- Ceiling space housing birds', rats' or possums' nests.
- Dusty ceiling space.

**Ignition in the ceiling space
is a major cause of house destruction and the deaths of shelterers.
Even a spark can ignite roof dust.
This eventually burns the rafters, the ceiling falls in and up goes the whole house.**

Roofing – protective

Best protection

- Material that allows the least airflow through it.
- No gaps in it.
- Non-flammable eaves and gutters.
    - ➢ Leaf-filled or plastic gutters can spread fire to interior of roof.
- Insulation batts between ridge and metal sheeting or under tiles.
- Nail holes soldered.
- Cyclone clips to prevent roof-lift in extreme wind conditions.

Roofing material

Best protection

- Strong, continuous, flat-troughed corrugated steel without ridge capping.
    - ➢ Minimises possibility of ember entry.
    - ➢ Has the strength to withstand falling-tree impact and gale-force wind.
    - ➢ Wide flat corrugations allow debris to roll off more easily than do rounded types.

Good protection

- Slate or fibre-cement tiles.
    - ➢ Fitted closely.
    - ➢ Kept free of cracks.
    - ➢ Underlaid with non-flammable insulation.
    - ➢ With boxed eaves.

Poor protection

- Tiles of terracotta, concrete or metal.
    - ➢ Gaps between them are common.
    - ➢ Can lift in strong winds and let in sparks.

Roofing material – hazardous

- Timber shingles are the most hazardous roofing possible.
    - ➢ Easily ignite from small sparks.
    - ➢ Ignited shingles pop off like corks and start more fires.
    - ➢ Ignited shingles stay alight even after long soaking in water.
    - ➢ Hot roofing nails burn holes in the shingle, allowing sparks access to rafters.

- Corrugated iron that does not fit snugly.
- Fibre-cement sheeting that is old and crumbly.

Roof pitch data

- Some authorities now favour an arced contour.

Roof pitch – protective

- Low-angled.
  - ➢ A gentle angle will carry a firewind over the house and away.
  - ➢ Allows ground-level observation of entire roof surface for landing embers.
  - ➢ A 15° angle limits fire-feeding air space between roofing and ceiling.
  - ➢ 15° is enough to allow a person into ceiling space to check for smouldering.
  - ➢ Tiled, metal and cement sheeting roofs can be constructed at 15°.

Roof pitch – hazardous

- Multiple pitches, gables and split levels.
  - ➢ Increase wind turbulence.
  - ➢ Embers can be hidden in the hips and hollows.
  - ➢ Leaves and burning debris collect in valleys and breaks in roof pitch.
  - ➢ Difficult to observe valleys.
- Angled junctions with carport, verandah or pergola.
  - ➢ Can be overcome by raising roof-line of appendage to meet line of main roof
  or
  - ➢ covering joint angle with non-combustible material such as sheet metal
  or
  - ➢ detaching appendage roof to create a gap.

Roof style – hazardous

- Rafter ends protruding externally.
  - ➢ Ceiling space fires often start from ignited rafter ends.
  - ➢ For safety, box in with non-combustible material
  or
  - ➢ coat with fire-retardant paint.

Roof ventilators (whirligigs)

- Enclose with metal mesh flywire.

Roof cyclone clips

- Can hold roof in place in winds of 150 km/h.

Roof sprinklers – protective

Best protection

- Low-flow type that allows water to run down over roof and walls.
  - ➢ Spray from butterfly and misting sprinklers is blown away by strong wind.
- Brass, low-flow spray nozzle heads. (See Chapter 13, Water for protection, 'A well-designed sprinkler system')

Gutters collect enough leaves and twigs on a dry windy day to cause severe fire risk. They can be left off some houses.

Gutters – protective

- Concrete or metal.
- Concrete gutter and lintel beams combined.
- Fitted with leaf protectors.

Gutters – hazardous

- Plastic.
  - ➢ Can warp in intense heat.
- Situated mid-house rather than around perimeter, like a valley between roof angles.
  - ➢ Hard to clear of leaves.
  - ➢ Hidden from sight so hard to defend from embers.
  - ➢ Don't stay filled with water to help protect roof.

Gutter alternatives

- Underground rubble drains that carry water to underground tanks.

Downpipes – protective

- Metal.

Downpipes – hazardous

- Plastic.
    - Can warp in intense heat.

Fascias and barge moulds – protective

- Well-painted timber.
- Cement sheeting at least 6 mm thick.
- Metal.
- Sealed fascias.
    - Can prevent sparks from entering the ceiling space.

Eaves – protective

Best protection

- No eaves.
    - Eaves are spark traps and difficult to seal.
    - They can, however, give windows useful protection from summer sun.

Next best protection

- Eaves boxed in at a 90° angle to the house with horizontal 6 mm lining boards.
    - Lining board insulated with fibreglass batts.
- Eaves fixed to roof with fire-rated eave and roof-profile filler strips.

Eaves – hazardous

- Acute-angled eaves that continue the rafter line.
    - These draw sparks to eave/wall joint.
- Plastic lining board.
    - Warps in heat to expose house frame and roofing timbers.

Chimneys and fireplaces – protective

- Chimney-top opening covered with metal flywire.
- Chimney with internal dampers and spark arresters.
- Fireplace with tight-fitting metal screen.
  - ➢ Embers that enter chimney won't fall into the room.

Chimneys and fireplaces – hazardous

- Uncovered chimney-top.
  - ➢ Allows embers to fall into fireplace.
- Unscreened fireplace.
  - ➢ Allows embers to roll into room and ignite furnishings.

Verandahs, carports and pergolas – protective

- Roof-line continuous with that of house roof, or separated from it by a wide gap.
- Pergolas uncovered – free of fibreglass sheeting or creeper.
  - ➢ Make fibreglass roofing or creeper safer by covering with metal flywire.
- Floor of earth, gravel, concrete, paving, brick, stone, slate or tiles.
- Timber floors smooth 25 mm hardwood: jarrah, red gum, mountain ash, merbau.
  - ➢ Unoiled.
  - ➢ Could be coated with fire-retardant paint.
- Supports of masonry or metal.
- Timber supports covered with insulation for 1 m from ground level.
- Roll-down metal shutter over openings.

Verandahs, carports and pergolas – hazardous

- Roof-line below that of house roof, forming an angle.
  - ➢ Can be overcome by raising roof-line to meet line of main roof
  or
  - ➢ covering juncture with non-combustible material such as sheet metal
  or
  - ➢ detaching appendage roof to create a gap.
- Pergolas roofed with plastic sheeting or shade-mesh.
  - ➢ Melt in sizzling drops which can give a nasty burn.
- Pergolas covered with creeper.
  - ➢ Can catch and hold embers against frame.
- Trellis or latticework.
  - ➢ Can catch embers.

Decks and steps – protective

Best protection

- Floor and treads of paving, brick or cement.
- Posts of metal or masonry.
- Exposed timber posts insulated with 6 mm non-combustible board or sheet steel.
- Under-area of raised deck surrounded with non-combustible material or metal flywire.
  - ➢ And bare of vegetation.
- Steps of concrete, brick or stone.

Good protection

- Floor and treads smooth 25 mm hardwood: jarrah, red gum, mountain ash, merbau.
  - ➢ Unoiled.
  - ➢ Could be coated with fire-retardant paint.
- Timber floor and treads separated from vertical wall by gap or metal grate.
  Or
- Joint angle covered with metal sheeting.
- Gapped timber decking boards covered with fine metal mesh.

Decks and steps – hazardous

- Timber decking floor and step treads abutting flammable vertical wall.
- Decking timber with gaps that can hold embers.
  - ➢ Could be protected by covering with fine metal mesh.
- Decking preserved with asphalt, tar or resinous coatings.
- Decking preserved with copper-chrome-arsenate salt.
  - ➢ Releases toxic arsenic gas when burning.

Vents and cracks

- Cover with fine metal flywire
  or
- fill with expandable fire-resistant sealant.

Firewood storage boxes

- Metal or brick, and draught-stopped, if part of the house.

Electricity meter box

- Metal.

Survival kit storage cupboard

- Can be on verandah or in laundry, hallway or kitchen.
- If outside:
  - ➤ On leeward side of the house.
  - ➤ Well-insulated and draught-stripped.
- A hook on wall beside the cupboard can hold an extension ladder for ceiling space access.

Laundry

- Fit an extra tap to which a hose is kept attached throughout summer.

Water tanks

- Metal or concrete.
  - ➤ Plastic tanks melt when exposed to embers or severe heat.

> **A fenceless home gives a bushfire free and easy access to your garden.**
> **Solid, non-flammable fences can stop the run of a surface fire**
> **and reduce the amount of radiant heat that reaches the house.**

House fences – protective

- Stone, brick or masonry.
  - ➤ Can halt approaching flames from forest and grass fire.
  - ➤ Protect from radiant heat.
- Colorbond® or corrugated metal.
- Cement sheeting.
- Chain mesh grown over with low-flammability creeper.
  - ➤ Can hinder fire approaching from mild bush, grass or crops.

House fences – hazardous

- Timber.
  - ➤ Uprights readily burn, crossbeams catch embers.
- Oiled timber is highly flammable.
- Timber treated with copper-chrome-arsenate salt exudes toxic gas when burning.

Free-standing ornamental walls

- Can be used as radiant heat shields.
  - ➤ Of non-flammable material.
  - ➤ At least 3 m wide and 2 m high.
  - ➤ Oriented at right angle to firewind direction.

Farm fences – protective

- Stone fences around paddocks can stop crop and grass fires.
  - ➤ The lives of thousands of stock can be saved this way.
- Metal or concrete drops for fence supports won't burn and collapse.
  - ➤ Metal drops stayed upright and intact on a ridge in Strathewen on Black Saturday.
- Metal flywire between bottom wire and ground can hinder the spread of a grass fire.

Farm fences – hazardous

- Wire fences with timber posts.
  - ➤ Posts burn and fencing wire then collapses.
  - ➤ To avoid collapse, drop metal 'star pickets' between timber posts.
- The older the timber, the drier and more flammable.
- Galvanised wire used in timber fences breaks down in fire and later rusts through.
- Holes bored through timber posts for wiring can catch sparks.
- Treated pine posts ignite at ground level and smoulder upwards.

Gates – protective

- Solid construction.
  - ➤ Wind cannot blow through and funnel the fire.
- Open design covered with metal flywire.
  - ➤ Burning debris will not roll through.
- Wide enough for a fire tanker to enter.
- Painted white, will be clearly seen by the fire service.

Outbuildings, sheds and garages – protective

- Metal roller doors.
  Or
- Solid, well-sealed, fire-rated doors.
- Metal or other shutters on windows. (See 'Shutters', above)
  Or
- Metal mesh on the outside of windows, all openings and cracks.
- No windows on fireward sides.
- Non-combustible 1 m base surround protects walls from grass fire or burning debris. (See 'Subfloor or subdeck surrounds', above)

**Even unattended hobby farms and holiday homes can survive
with these protective features.**

10
Protective furnishings

Furnishing fabric determines

- Whether an ember or running flame will ignite the padding beneath it.

Furnishing padding determines

- Whether the furnishing will continue to burn.
- How soon flame follows after smouldering.
- Whether the furniture structure beneath will burn.
- How quickly flame leaps from it to ignite other items.
- Intensity of heat generated.
- Amount of smoke.
- Whether poisonous gas is given off.

Furnishings – protective

- A spark or ember that lands on it will die out.
- Any flame generated in it moves slowly.
  - ➢ Giving time to extinguish, or escape from, the fire.
- Natural padding has low flammability.

Furnishings – hazardous

- A spark or ember that lands on it flares quickly.
- Any flame generated in it moves quickly.
  - ➤ Accelerating spread to other furniture and the house structure.
- When heated gives off toxic fumes.
  - ➤ This quickly endangers life.

Furnishing fabrics – protective

Cannot be ignited by flame

- Pure, untreated, heavy-quality wool.
- Natural leather.
- Good-quality vinyl.

Cannot be ignited by an ember

- Pure, untreated, heavy-quality wool.
- Natural leather.
- Good-quality vinyl.
  - ➤ Embers smoulder slowly and usually die out.

Will only burn if kept in constant contact with flame

- Modified acrylic.
  - ➤ The chemicals used in modacrylic give it flame retardant properties.

A bushfire's embers and flames can cause house *ignitions*.
But the *total destruction* of houses is caused by the untended burning of its contents.

Furnishing fabrics and components – hazardous

Can be ignited by an ember

- Cotton, rayon, linen, unmodified acrylic.

Can be ignited by a flame

- Cotton, rayon, linen.
- The plastic coating of fibreglass fabrics.
- Unmodified acrylic.
  - ➤ Gives off thick black smoke.
  - ➤ Creates burning molten drips.
- Nylon, terylene, dacron and other synthetics.
  - ➤ Create molten drips.

Can be ignited by a small flame if the covering fabric allows it

- Polyurethane foam padding.
  - ➤ Burns fast.
  - ➤ Gives off more smoke and gases than natural padding.
  - ➤ When smouldering, gives off lethal toxic fumes.

Give off toxic fumes

- Polyurethane foam padding.
  - ➤ Gives off cyanide gas when smouldering.
- Synthetic materials and plastics.
  - ➤ Give off cyanide gas when burning.

When an unattended spark or ember from bushfire is blown inside a house, it smoulders, flares, and fire spreads through furniture and furnishings, clothes and kitchen contents, papers and plastics and fly-sprays and cleaning fluids until only ash and twisted metal remain.

Furnishings – amount and placement

- Cluttered furnishings help flame spread.
- Furnishings close to windows are vulnerable to entering embers.
- Furnishings placed close to flammable curtains can be ignited by them.
- Flammable curtains can ignite ceilings.

Floor coverings – protective

- Slate, tile, brick or pure wool.
  - ➤ Embers landing on them self-extinguish.

Bedding – protective

- Bedspreads and quilts of pure wool.
- Quilts and pillows of down or feathers.
  - ➢ For protection, outer cover must also be non-flammable.

Bedding – hazardous

- Covers of cotton or synthetic.
- Covers with button depressions or rolled edges.
  - ➢ Could trap sparks.
- Blankets of unmodified acrylic and cotton.
- Sheets of cotton and synthetic.
- Mattresses with natural padding.
  - ➢ Ignite from embers.
- Mattresses with foam padding.
  - ➢ Ignite from small flames.
  - ➢ Give off more smoke than those of inner-spring.
  - ➢ Can give off toxic gas.

Other furnishing hazards

- Curtains that are light-reflecting.
  - ➢ Polymers in them increase the heat and smoke given off.
- Cushions loosely fitted to chairs and lounge suites.
  - ➢ Allow embers to lodge unseen between them and arm or back of the item.
- Chairs that are linen-covered or polyurethane-padded.
  - ➢ Embers landing on these emit lethal cyanide gas within 30 seconds.
- Beanbags and cushions filled with polyurethane beads.
  - ➢ If cover is damaged, heated beads scatter as multiple toxic gas emitters.
- Air conditioning units.
  - ➢ Allow spark entry.
  - ➢ When components ignite, burning plastic beads pour into rooms through vents.
  - ➢ Conduits channel fumes throughout the house.

Be aware of which aspect of your house can contribute most to its destruction: not the cladding, the contents!

11

Shelters, refuges and bunkers

A home bushfire shelter should be only one aspect of protective preparations.
The safety record of shelters is far from perfect and can give an unfounded sense of security.
Be aware of their limitations.
You still need to reduce fuel, fortify your house against ember entry and act safely.

A bushfire shelter can be

1 A community shelter provided by authorities for residents and visitors.
2 A personal shelter provided by householders on their own property.

1 A community shelter provided by authorities can be

- A building specially constructed to withstand ember penetration and violent wind.
- A public building modified with protective features.
- A large tunnel.
- An open space such as a sports ground, park or beach.
  - ➢ This is the least suitable.
  - ➢ Neighbourhood Safer Places are not deemed to be shelters or refuges.
    (See Chapter 15, Township protection)

Community shelters – protective aim

- Protection for a large number of vulnerable residents, visitors and tourists.
  - ➢ It is very difficult for municipalities to provide enough suitable shelters.

Community shelters need

- Well-marked, short routes to them that are safe for travel in bushfire conditions.
- Space to accommodate local evacuees plus tourists.

- Access early on each day of announced bushfire danger and for its duration.
- Site cleared of flammable vegetation for at least 40 m.
- Site entirely cleared of combustible mulch.
- Solid building with protected windows and doors, secure roofs and sheltered exits.
- Roof able to withstand winds over 150 km/h and secured with cyclone clips.
- Metal roll-down window shutters.
- Metal roll-down door shutters
  or
- fire-rated solid-core doors with metal mesh screens and draught-stoppers.
- Non-flammable furnishings and wall linings that do not emit toxic gases when heated.
- Ventilation that does not admit smoke.
- Mesh covers over skylights and roof-mounted air conditioner units.
- Roof and ground sprinklers.
- Large reserve water supply, independent of mains pressure.
- Facilities for water, food and rest.
- Amenities for babies and the frail.
- Shade and water for pets.
- Sufficient toilets.
- Provision of fire-safe blankets (preferably pure wool) for last-resort protection.
- First aid and firefighting equipment.
- Sufficient parking clear of flammable trees, grass and woodchips.

Benefits of community shelters

- Relatively safe places for:
  - ➢ Those with demonstrably undefendable houses.
  - ➢ Those too fearful to defend their home.
- Shelterers may have the protection of firefighters.
- Shelterers may have more shelter than at home.
- Shelterers will have company.

Hazards of community shelters

- Outlying evacuees can be endangered while travelling to them.
- Buildings designated as shelters may not be of suitable construction.
- Open spaces designated as shelters may be grassy and adjoin flammable vegetation.
- Open spaces leave evacuees exposed to embers, firebrands, smoke and weather.
- May not have water available for drinking, ablutions or defence.
- May not have space to accommodate local evacuees plus tourists.
- May not have facilities for food and rest or amenities for babies and the frail.
- May not have sufficient toilets or parking.
- May not have room for pets.

> Survival prospects in a private bushfire shelter depend equally on
> * good design and construction   * the behaviour of shelterers.
> Ill-informed or incautious use severely cuts shelterers' survival chances.

2 Personal shelters provided by householders can be

A. An external structure such as a bunker or dugout.
B. A part of the house modified and reinforced as a refuge room.

Personal shelters – protective aim

- To remove the worry of evacuating vulnerable family members with little warning.
- To remove the need to evacuate defenders if house becomes endangered.

A. External structures such as bunkers and dugouts

Bunkers and dugouts need

- Design and construction that conform to latest Australian Standard specifications.
    - ➤ A building permit is required to install or construct a private bushfire shelter.
- To be large enough for the number of occupants likely to use the building.
- Entrance protected by a three-sided, 2 m radiant heat shield about 5 m from it.
- A sheltered exit door from the house.
- Wide access path clear of vegetation, litter and debris.
- Allowance for topography, vegetation, adjacent buildings, site size and fire intensity.
- To be sited well away from the house and trees that could fall on it.
- No flammable matter for at least 10 m around it.
- A means of identifying shelterers' existence and whereabouts, for rescue purposes.

Inside, they need

- Non-flammable furnishings and fittings that do not emit toxic gases if heated.
- Ventilation with the ability to keep the shelter smoke-free.
    - ➤ People have died in bunkers undamaged by fire, killed by infiltrating toxic gases.
- No normal windows.
- A small, wire-reinforced lookout window.
- Provision of drinking water.
- Provision of toilet facilities.
- Provision of pure wool blankets, and nose masks.
- Provision of first aid and firefighting equipment.

Benefits of personal shelters such as bunkers and dugouts

- Ideal for storage of precious possessions and pets.
- An alternative to evacuation for
    - ➢ The very young, old and frail.
    - ➢ Those too fearful to defend the home.
- A relatively safe place for home defenders as a retreat of last resort.

Hazards of personal shelters, bunkers and dugouts

- Lack of safe access, difficult entry and exit facility.
- Flammable vegetation or materials nearby.
- Neglect of maintenance of shelter and environs.
- Not suitable for those unable to stay confined in a small space.
- Little is known at present on how shelters perform during a bushfire.
- Difficult to get ventilation right to prevent both smoke inhalation and suffocation.
- Steel exteriors of shipping containers can get glowing hot and overheat interior.
- Concrete cylinders and septic tanks get hot and airless due to low body:space ratio.
    - ➢ Shelterers in these can suffer dehydration, fainting, heat exhaustion or heat stroke.

Hazards of both public and personal bushfire shelters come mostly from

- Making poor decisions before and during a fire.
    - ➢ Accessing the shelter too late, leaving too soon or staying in it too long.
- Too many occupants for size of shelter.

**Realise that while you shelter in a community refuge or private bunker
your deserted house is more vulnerable to destruction.**

B. Part of the house modified and reinforced as a refuge room

Refuge room – protective aim

- To do away with the need to worry about evacuation of the very young or frail.
- To greatly increase your chance of saving the house safely.
- A readily accessible and safe retreat if your house ignites while defending it.

A refuge room can be

- Included in an original house plan.
- Added on.
- Part of an existing house modified to double as a refuge room.
- Included in business premises and institutions for protection of employees.

In existing house – possible adaptations

- A small, strong room built onto the leeward side of the house.
- A soundly constructed room that is easy to enter and leave safely.
- An adjoining brick garage.
- A laundry. (See *The Complete Bushfire Safety Book*, Chapter 9, Facilities for bushfire defence, 'A safe refuge room')

A refuge room needs

- Separation from the main house by a heavily insulated wall of brick or concrete.
- Connecting door to interior of the house of solid-core timber, fire-rated
  or
- insulated with heavy cement-sheeting layer between two timber layers.
  - ➤ Weather-stripped and fitted with draught-stoppers.
- Exit door of solid-core timber, fire-rated
  or
- insulated with heavy cement-sheeting layer between two timber layers.
  - ➤ Weather-stripped.
  - ➤ With shielding metal mesh screen door.
  - ➤ Opening to courtyard, low-flammability garden or fallow paddock.
  - ➤ Protected by radiant heat shield no more than 5 m from it.
- Ceiling of reinforced concrete
  or
- timber reinforced and insulated.
  - ➤ Double-layered 'fire-stop' plasterboard above and below.
  - ➤ Sandwiched-in 100 mm² mesh to protect from falling materials.
- Separation of refuge room roof space from main roof space by heavily insulated barrier.
- Separate ceiling space inspection trapdoor.
- Roof able to withstand wind of 150 km/h and secured with cyclone clips.
- Floor of concrete
  or
- insulated timber. (See Chapter 9, A protective house design)
  - ➤ Outer walls strongly constructed of low-flammability materials, well-insulated.
- At least 2 m bare space between outer walls and flammable vegetation.

- A spyglass in the outer door
  or
- a small lookout window, reinforced with wire mesh.
  - ➤ Through which to monitor fire behaviour.
- Any normal windows protected with metal shutters operated from the inside.
- An internal water supply with hose permanently attached to a reserve tap.
- Ventilation that does not allow sparks or smoke to enter.
  - ➤ Inner door can be left open to the air of house until retreat to refuge needed.
- Any flammable, explosive or toxicity-producing contents removed.

Benefits of refuge rooms

As for bunkers, with the addition of

- More comfort, easier access to water and food for shelterers.
- Allows defenders to readily check on early shelterers.
- Needs of very young and old more easily met.
- Safe and readily accessible retreat for both shelterers and home defenders.
  - ➤ Does away with dangers of exposure during an external retreat.

Hazards of refuge rooms

- Large or unprotected windows.
- Poor ventilation.
- Construction not strong enough.
- Exit door facing a steep, vegetated slope.
- Exit door leading to flammable steps.

Hazards of cellars

- Extremely hazardous as shelters.
  - ➤ Burning floorboards above a cellar can ignite and trap shelterers.
  - ➤ A gutted house can fall inwards into cellar or storeroom.
  - ➤ Toxic gases from burning substances can infiltrate.

Hazards of foil tents

- Direct flame contact or embers can burn holes in foil.
- Foil cannot filter smoke.
- Foil does not 'breathe', so sweating and high body temperature can occur.
- Lack of ventilation while under foil can cause loss of consciousness.

Emergency shelters

- Car parked in a cleared area.
- Swimming pool, dam or river, if clear of vegetation.
- Public toilet block built of stone or brick.
- Cave or tunnel.
- A large, closely woven, pure wool blanket.
    - Pure wool protects from radiant heat.
    - Pure wool is not burnt by embers.
    - Wool filters smoke.
- A foil tent.
    - Foil can protect from radiant heat.

Of the 172 who died in the 2009 Black Saturday fires, 8% chose very hazardous shelters: sheds, subfloor bunkers and even spas on timber decks.
Some shelters resisted fire but killed their occupants by allowing toxic gases to enter.

12
Protective equipment

Bushfires have been beaten away from buildings with no better equipment than green branches and wet bags.
But the more protective equipment you have,
the better chance of you and your home surviving a bushfire.

The personal survival kit

- This is a satchel or bag of protective clothing and accessories.
  - ➢ Prepare it well before the bushfire season.
  - ➢ Keep it in a specially allocated place, such as hall, laundry or verandah cupboard.
  - ➢ Take it with you whenever you travel into bushfire territory.
- Having this available can make the difference between your life and death.

Survival kit – protective clothing

- Boiler suit of heavy-duty cotton-drill
  - ➢ Tight weave, high neckline, no waistband, long sleeves and legs, firm cuffs.
  - ➢ Legs and sleeves neither tight nor flared.
  Or
- long, straight-legged trousers.
  - ➢ Strong cotton or pure wool.
  - ➢ Neither tight nor flared.
- Strong drill shirt which buttons up to the neck
  or
- long-sleeved, pure wool, neck-hugging pullover.
  - ➢ Not cowl or polo neck.
  - ➢ Neither tight nor flared.

- Underwear of cotton.
  - ➢ Not nylon or polyester.
- A hard hat

  or
- strong, wide-brimmed, heavy cotton or felt hat that can be tied on
  - ➢ Not straw

  or
- strong cotton scarf or woollen cap that completely covers your hair.
- Strong leather boots or shoes.
  - ➢ Soles of thick nitrone rubber.
  - ➢ No hobnails.
- Pure wool socks.
- Strong gardening gloves made of canvas.
  - ➢ For protection when moving hot objects. (See Chapter 3, The survival factors)

Survival kit clothes

Protective ways to wear

- Light and loose-fitting to let you sweat.
- Hats tied on.
- Shirts and pullovers tucked into trousers.
  - ➢ So sparks cannot be blown up inside them to burn your chest.
- Trousers tucked firmly into socks.
  - ➢ So heat or flame won't run up inside them to burn your legs or pelvic area.
- Trouser legs tied firmly over boots at the ankle.
  - ➢ So embers can't drop into boots.

Hazardous

- Light cotton, synthetics, loose or fuzzy weave.
  - ➢ Ignite easily.
- Heavy material.
  - ➢ Will tire you.
- Short trousers.
- Tight-cut, close-fitting jeans.
  - ➢ Embers landing on them can burn through to your skin.
- Skirts or flared trousers.
  - ➢ Flames can flare under them and burn your body.
- Tight waistbands.
  - ➢ Can constrict blood circulation.

- Loose pullover or shirt.
  - ➤ Flames can reach up to burn skin or underwear.
- Short or no sleeves.
  - ➤ Embers can land on arms.
- Flared sleeves.
  - ➤ Flame can reach inside.
- Loose or cowl necks.
  - ➤ Embers can be caught in them.
- Thongs, plastic shoes or shoes with hobnails (See Chapter 2, The killer factors, 'Clothing')
- Nylon underwear.

The most suitable clothes are strong enough for radiant heat protection, as well as comfortable and adjustable to allow sweat to evaporate and cool you.

Survival kit accessories

- Sturdy, tightly woven pure wool blanket or textured fibreglass throw-over
  - ➤ Large enough to cover you completely when crouched or lying down.
  - Or
- heavy-duty aluminium foil tent.
  - ➤ Protects from radiant heat but not from flames or embers.
- Bottles for drinking water.
- Gel necktie cooler and/or gel vest.
- Smoke-filtering nose cover.
  - ➤ A non-synthetic scarf, tea-towel, large handkerchief
  - or
  - ➤ mask that will filter particles of 0.01 micron.
- Water in containers for damping homemade nose cover.
  - ➤ A small spray bottle is useful.
- Bottle of artificial tears or gel.
  - ➤ To avoid drying of eyes and grit irritation.
- Wide-vision goggles with vent, or wrap-around sunglasses.
- Strap to tie glasses on in high wind.
- Demisting device to prevent fogging.
- Ultra-violet reflective suncream (such as zinc) to protect forehead and nose.
- First aid kit. (See Chapter 23, First aid for bushfire injuries)

Survival kit – pets

- Pure wool or leather back-coat for dog.
  - ➤ To keep sparks and embers out of fur.
- Small pure wool blanket to cover bird cage or cat cage.
- Foil, pure wool or textured fibreglass blanket to drape over an aviary.

**With a pure wool blanket,
people and pets have survived the most extreme bushfires.**

Firefighting equipment

- Reserve water. (See Chapter 13, Water for protection)
  - ➤ Don't rely on mains water supply. This often fails during a bushfire.
- Optional foam additive for water.
  - ➤ Can increase water's effectiveness and decrease the amount needed.
- Non-electric water pump.
  - ➤ Electricity supply can fail during a bushfire.
  - ➤ Most reliable are generators, diesel or those that function by gravity flow.
- Stirrup pump, knapsack sprayers with pump.
- Garden sprayers.
  - ➤ More accurate than bucket-throw, use less water and cause less body strain.
- Water containers from which to replenish sprayers.
  - ➤ Utilise metal buckets, drums, old baths, wash troughs.
  - ➤ Place at vulnerable spots around and in house.
- Mops, dippers for throwing water from containers.
- Hoses of rubber or flat canvas up to 30 m long.
  - ➤ Water pressure can fall in longer hoses.
- Enough standpipes so that 30 m hoses can reach any part of the property.
- Nozzle-activated hose jets.
- Hose connectors.
- Fire extinguishers.
  - ➤ Foam, carbon dioxide or dry chemical for fires fuelled by grease, oil or petrol.
- Beaters of thonged leather or canvas, or hessian bags.
- Rakes, rakehoes, shovels.

> Don't rely solely on sophisticated fire equipment. You need back-ups.
> Pumps and fire hoses that were checked and working the night before,
> can fail during an emergency.

Equipment accessories

- Extension ladder and stepladder.
- Ploughs, graders and rotary hoes.
  - ➤ For creating earth barriers and emergency ditches.
- Listening set linked to local rural fire brigade, two-way portable radio, mobile phone.
- Battery-operated radio for listening to bushfire news bulletins.
  - ➤ Electricity often fails during a bushfire emergency.
- Shrill whistle for emergency signalling to family members.
- Torches and batteries.
- Pure wool blankets.
- Fibreglass blankets (such as Firestop).
- Tennis balls, milk carton bottoms or commercial devices for plugging downpipes.

Equipment – hazardous

- Water put on grease, oil or petrol fires.
- Tap-stands set against buildings.
  - ➤ If the building ignites you might not be able to access the tap.
- Plastic water tanks.
- Plastic hoses.
- Plastic buckets.
- Plastic tap fittings.
  - ➤ Plastic can melt in an intense bushfire.
  - ➤ With suitable fuel reduction around the house, this will not happen.

> A fit person, protectively clothed, armed with a smoke mask, mop, sprayer
> and 1000 L of water (about four 44 gallon drums or seven baths' full)
> should be well able to defend their house against ember ignition by most bushfires.

13
Water for protection

The reason many people lose their homes to bushfire,
despite having carried out otherwise good preparations,
is because they have no reserve water supply.

Three core aspects of water for protection from bushfire

- Independent, reliable source of supply.
- Kept for fire-fighting only.
- Enough to protect your property in your environmental circumstances.

Water supply must be

- Calculated to suit house size and design, proximity, density and type of vegetation.
  (See 'Reserve water requirements', below)
- Organised with a special reserve supply for bushfire use only.
- Stored in a metal, not plastic, tank.
  - ➤ Plastic tanks melt during severe bushfire.
- Carried in metal pipes.
  - ➤ Can be plastic if underground.
- Protected from radiant heat.
- Used in the most effective way. (See Chapter 21, What to do when bushfire threatens)

Reserve water is necessary because

- You need an assured supply of water.
  - ➤ Mains water pressure falls during bushfire when fire units use it.
  - ➤ It also falls when tap fittings on the same mains line are burnt or melted.
  - ➤ Often mains water is cut completely.
- Vital to have available for quick dousing of embers and ignitions.

Reserve water requirements

- Houses and small businesses, at least 1000 L (more for sprinklers – see below).
- Large properties, at least 17 500 L. (See *The Complete Bushfire Safety Book*, Chapter 9, Facilities for bushfire defence)

Take into account

- Size of protection area, building design, local vegetation type and density.
- Proximity, density and type of vegetation.
  - ➤ This can indicate potential intensity and duration of a fire.
  - ➤ Therefore how much water flow could be needed per minute and for how long.

(See 'Calculating sprinkler system water requirements', below.)

Reserve water supply can be held in

- Tank.
  - ➤ Mains water can be run into a reserve tank, to keep it always full.
- Dam.
- Pond.
- Swimming pool.

Reserve tank requirements

- A separate tank kept strictly for firefighting
  - ➤ Clearly marked 'RESERVE FIREWATER'.
  - or
- a general household tank modified with:
  - ➤ A second tap inserted at the halfway level.
  - ➤ The normal tap at the base marked 'RESERVE FIREWATER'.
  - ➤ From the top tap, draw water from the upper half of the tank for household use.
  - ➤ From the bottom tap, draw water from the lower half of the tank for fire-fighting.

- All tanks should be fitted with:
  - ➢ Large outlet, gate valve and a coupling to which fire-tanker hose can be connected.
  - ➢ Connection to taps inside the house.

Reserve water tank – best types

- Underground.
- Concrete or metal if above ground.

Reserve water supply – layout

- Within the inner zone of protection. (See Chapter 7, A protective property layout)
- At each building and outbuilding.
  - ➢ On their leeward sides.
- Gravity-fed supply sited higher than building.

A gravity-fed water supply can be

- Tank, dam or swimming pool on slope above the house.
  - ➢ At least 25 m higher than intended destination of water.
- Tank raised on a stand so that it is high above house.

All raised tank stands must be

- Kept clear underneath.
- Protected with non-flammable surround.

Water pipes must be

- Metal
  or
- plastic pipes laid 40 cm underground.
  - ➢ Plastic can melt if subjected to high heat.

Water pumps must be

- Non-electric.
  - ➤ Electric water pumps can fail during bushfire.
  - ➤ Authorities may disconnect power during bushfire as a precaution.

Water pumps – protective

- Generator-powered
  or
- portable, easy to start, self-priming petrol or diesel motor 3.7 kW (5 HP).
  - ➤ Pump HP depends on degree of risk, sprinkler needs and spray head type.
- Housed in a non-flammable shelter with metal mesh-covered vents.
- Fitted with a fine screen on the suction.
- Permanently connected to non-gravity fed reserve water supply.
- Supplied with at least two hours' fuel.
  - ➤ Pre-test for fuel running time and top up before fuel is likely to run out.
  - ➤ Refill fuel tins stored near pump must be in non-flammable housing.
    (See Chapter 7, A protective property layout, 'Fuel')

Sprinklers should not be looked upon as an all-in-one bushfire defence strategy. But they can ease the difficult physical problems of home defenders.

Sprinklers

A well-designed sprinkler system can

- Protect house, garden and other important assets.
- Decrease your energy output during an emergency.
- Decrease the need for vegetation clearance in environmentally sensitive areas.
- Negate the need for some aspects of house modification.
- Negate the need for evacuation.

Main areas in need of sprinkler protection

- Flammable walls.
- Windows.
- Decks.
- Roof valleys.
- Galvanised iron roofs.
- Tiled roofs.
- Cement-sheeting roofs.
- Eaves.
- Gutters.
- Skylights
- Air conditioning unit intakes.
- Roof whirligigs.
- Refuge room or bunker.
- Exit doors.
- Gardens.

Other areas for sprinkler protection

- Stockyards.
- Stables.
- Milking sheds.
- Aviaries.
- Fowl pens.
- Fauna sanctuaries, pet boarding facilities.
- Garages.
- Sheds.
- Fuel tanks.
- LP gas cylinders.
- Machinery.
- Perimeter fences.
- Radiant heat shields.

Areas that don't need sprinkler protection

- Blank brick walls.
- Continuous metal roofing.

Before installing a sprinkler system

- Analyse your house and garden's specific risks.
  - ➤ Discuss your needs with a bushfire sprinkler specialist.
  - ➤ Ascertain how much water flow will be needed per minute and for how long.

Sprinkler system design

- Most protective when water is run down over roof and walls like a waterfall.
  - ➤ Spray flung from a roof ridge can be blown away by typically violent winds.
- Spray nozzle heads must be brass to withstand heat.
- The potential threat to an individual property will determine:
  - ➤ Type of spray heads.
  - ➤ Placement of spray heads.
  - ➤ Water supply needed.
  - ➤ Pump size and type.

Spray nozzle head requirements for house and various protective zones

- On roof, 180–360° low-flow spray nozzle heads to fully drench roof, eaves and walls.
- Around house,10 m ring of butterfly spray nozzle heads to protect garden.
- Further out, 30–40 m ring of impact spray nozzle heads to protect bushland.
  - ➤ Variety and deployment of sprinkler heads depends on the environment.

Calculating sprinkler system water requirements

Take into account

- Size of protection area.
- Severity of fire from which you expect to need protection.
  - ➤ Therefore how much water flow will be needed per minute and for how long.
- Amount of water supply.

- Estimated running time.
  - ➤ Allow for at least a half hour before, and four hours after, fire front arrival.
  - ➤ An hour's water supply is enough to protect from grass fire.
  - ➤ Forest fire protection needs more water, depending on vegetation density and type.
- Spray head type.
  - ➤ Some spray heads release water faster than others.
- 17 500 L of water will give you spray cover for one to two hours.
  - ➤ Depending on the size of system, flow rate, number and size of sprinkler heads.

When to use a sprinkler system

- During the shower of embers. (See Chapter 4, How bushfire destroys houses)
  - ➤ It is pointless and wasteful to turn it on before this.
- Do not run it for the entire duration of a perceived threat.
- Do not turn it on as you evacuate.
  - ➤ Sprinklers may have run out of water by the most vital time of need.

A makeshift sprinkler

- Attach a 40 mm metal water pipe to a fence.
  - ➤ Insert either metal butterfly spray heads or taps.

**Most people who have planned well and practised their plan,
who have a dependable water supply and understand what to do with it,
have a very good chance of saving their homes and themselves.**

14
Planning ahead

Stayers, goers and shelterers need equally to be prepared, planned and practised
– with a plan that includes knowing how to defend safely, how to leave safely –
how to leave the house so it can survive and how to shelter safely if it's too late to leave.

There are four core aspects of any bushfire safety plan

- The management of vegetation surrounding your house.
- The ember resistance of your house.
- Personal protection from radiant heat and heat stress.
- The knowledge of how to react safely to a bushfire threat.
    - ➢ Attention to one aspect alone can be dangerous. They must be woven together.

There are four core aspects to the plan to 'stay or go'

- Whole family to stay and defend.
- Partial family to defend, children and frail to shelter.
- Whole family to evacuate.
- Partial family to evacuate.
    - ➢ Children and frail to be moved to safety when bushfire weather is forecast.
    - ➢ The fit and knowledgeable to stay home to defend the property.

Whether you plan to defend, evacuate or shelter

- Think about every aspect of this book in relation to your property and capabilities.
- Read *The Complete Bushfire Safety Book* for an in-depth understanding.
- Read fire authority publications and books listed in the bibliography of this book.
- Find out costs of safety features. Draw up a budget. Check out cheaper alternatives.

- Discuss all these matters thoroughly with family and knowledgeable people.
- Discuss your proposed preparations with neighbours and local rural fire brigade.
  - ➢ 'I'm going to stay' or 'We're getting out' are not plans. They are headlines.
  - ➢ Plans for bushfire safety must be detailed, comprehensive and thorough.

Personal safety

- Prepare a detailed survival plan and become familiar with its aspects. (See Chapter 2, The killer factors, and Chapter 3, The survival factors)
- Put together a survival kit for every family member and pet. (See Chapter 12, Protective equipment)
- Mark on the calendar a date, before the bushfire season starts, to check and pack kits.
- Purchase pure wool blankets and smoke masks.
  - ➢ Heavy duty pure wool ex-army grey blankets may be found at disposal stores.
- Include children in both planning and practising of plans.
  - ➢ Through safety-aware children we build communities of safety-aware adults.
- Ascertain whether school holds children or sends them home for bushfire threats.
- Check if authorisation is needed for a person other than a parent to collect your children.
- If children are to be kept at home, plan how you will organise:
  - ➢ Your work schedule.
  - ➢ A carer, if unable to stay home yourself.
- Plan for extra drinking water bottles or flasks.
- Plan where to put pets during a bushfire threat.
- Practise wearing protective clothing and goggles, and breathing through mask.
- Discuss having an inbuilt refuge room or external bunker. (See Chapter 11, Shelters, refuges and bunkers)

Safety of pets

(See Chapter 16, Protective chores and Chapter 18, Protecting domestic animals, stock and sanctuaries)
- Plan where to put pets during a bushfire threat.
- Ascertain whether the local council has emergency shelter arrangements for animals.
- Obtain identity tags and/or microchip.
- Place your mobile number and vet's phone number on tag or registration database.
- Photograph pets and valuable stock.
  - ➢ Label the photographs.
  - ➢ Store them with your survival kit.

- Plan for friends or protected boarding in safe area to take pets ahead of risky days.
- Plan to get cat cages.
- Discuss having wall or low-flammability shrubs to shield kennels and fowl pens.
- Plan for safety of horses.

Safety of stock

- Discuss how and where to create a stock refuge. (See Chapter 16, Protective chores)
- Talk over with your family the safest time to herd stock into it.
    - ➢ Draw up a stock action plan from the points listed in Chapter 21.
    - ➢ Practise herding stock into their refuge. Get them used to it.
- Appoint someone as emergency musterer.

Safety of surrounding vegetation

Garden

- Plan what plants to thin out, move, remove or replace.
- Plan low-flammability vegetation to plant, and where.
- Discuss creation of gravel areas.
- Design protective paths between walls and garden.
- Plan where and how to build a radiant heat shield.
    - ➢ If brick is too expensive, think about earth mounds or low-flammability shrubs.
- Discuss replacing timber fences with a non-combustible type or low-flammability hedges.
- Plan reserve water supply, number of tanks, pumps, sprinkler installation.
    - ➢ If you can't afford sprinklers or tanks, the tip may have old baths and drums.
- Plan to replace plastic tanks with a metal or concrete type.
- Check how far hoses reach and whether more are needed.
- Are extra taps needed? Plan their positions.
- Check ladder-reach and that ladders are in safe condition.
- Discuss how you will monitor weather and observe smoke for danger signs.
- Practise studying nature's advance warning system. (See *The Complete Bushfire Safety Book*, Chapter 11, How to prepare for the bushfire season, 'Weather forecasts')

Farm

- Plan what vegetation to thin, remove or replace.
- Plan fuelbreaks and windbreaks. (See Chapter 7, A protective property layout)
  - ➢ What areas are to be intensively grazed, mowed or burnt?
  - ➢ What areas are to be sprayed to create fuelbreaks?
  - ➢ What areas are to be fallow?
- Discuss replacing or staggering timber fencing posts with metal drops.
- Decide if modifications are needed to sheds, hay and fuel storage.

Safety of house

- Walk around the house, note aspects that need repair, modification or replacement. (See Chapter 5, The home as a haven, and Chapter 9, A protective house design)
- Make a shopping list of requirements. Budget for firefighting equipment.
- Browse thrift shops for protective clothing and water containers, such as old troughs.
- Plan a timetable for chores so they'll be done before the bushfire season starts. (See Chapter 16, Protective chores)
- Plan how to clean out ceiling space.
  - ➢ Would it be easier in the long run to have it commercially cleaned?
- Get quotes for installation of ceiling, wall and subfloor insulation.
- Plan window protection. (See Chapter 9, A protective house design, or *The Complete Bushfire Safety Book*, Chapter 8, Design to keep bushfire out of buildings)
- Discuss replacing wall linings that could give off toxic fumes when burning.
- Examine roof and walls for holes and cracks. Budget for purchase and use of sealant.
- Get quotes for metal mesh and its installation over windows, subfloor and vents.
- Discuss whether leaf-free gutters are needed.
- Get quotes for roof sprinklers, window shutters.
  - ➢ Discuss needs with a bushfire sprinkler specialist.
- Estimate number of torches needed. Buy supply of batteries.

Safety of house contents

- Consider cost of replacing flammable furnishings with protective types.
  - ➢ And the potential cost of not replacing them. (See Chapter 10, Protective furnishings.)

Safety of precious possessions and important papers

- Plan what to relocate, where and at what stage.
  - ➤ For the duration of the bushfire season.
  - ➤ On a fire-danger day.
  - ➤ With a friend at a safe house in town
  - ➤ In a storage facility in town.
  - ➤ Buried in garden dugout in moisture-proof wraps.
- Consider whether large, unstorable valuables could be covered in insulation.
- Budget for an external hard drive and high-GB memory stick for your computer.

Safety of refuge room or bunker

- Reassess safety requirements. (See Chapter 11, Shelters, refuges and bunkers.)
  - ➤ Plan for stocking with blankets, water, hose, sprayers and first aid equipment.
- Reassess ventilation and smoke penetration.
- Obtain quotes for erection of radiant heat shield to protect entrance.
- Practise staying in it for 15–30 minutes in protective clothing, with pets.

Having a bushfire safety plan does work.
But it has to be thorough. It has to be based on the best knowledge.
And it has to be practised.

Safety for defence, shelter and evacuation

If you plan to defend your home

- Devise a bushfire safety action plan. (See Chapter 21, What to do when bushfire threatens)
- Practise plan frequently and become thoroughly familiar with all aspects.
  - ➤ Particularly useful is to practise on a hot, windy day to understand conditions.
- Practise accessing vulnerable areas of house that could catch embers.
- Practise water-reach of garden sprayers, knapsacks and bucket-throw.
- Note local weather patterns: watch to which side of house wind generally blows leaves.
  - ➤ This is where you can expect embers and burning debris to accumulate.
- Find out your state and local bushfire laws.
- Discuss at work the possibility of your staying home on fire-danger days.
- Discuss your plans with local bushfire brigade.

If you plan non-defensive shelter

- Prepare a bushfire sheltering plan and become familiar with all aspects. (See Chapter 20, Evacuate, defend or shelter? and Chapter 21, What to do when bushfire threatens, 'Safe sheltering procedure')
- Discuss house safety modifications, as above.
- Budget to provide enough pure wool blankets or foil tents.
- Discuss whether to construct a refuge room or bunker
  or
- whether you will simply shelter in the house.
- Decide which exit door would be the safest by which to shelter.
- Understand that for safe exit from an ignited house you need to:
  - ➤ Be protected by strong clothing, a smoke mask and a pure wool blanket.
  - ➤ Exit before flame, smoke or toxic gas spreads through the house.
  - ➤ But after the peak of flames outside the house has died down.
    - − This is why you need to have cleared flammable vegetation from near the house.
- Plan construction of a radiant heat shield to protect your chosen exit door.
- Plan where to go if the house has burnt, and how to get there safely.
- Plan whether to prepare any defensive equipment, such as water sprayers.
- Practise your sheltering technique, dressed in protective clothing.

**Post-Black Saturday research by bushfire scientists showed that
over a third of those who died sheltering had not known how to do so safely.
To shelter safely in the house, you must stay near an exit door.
Not in an inner room. Not in the bath.**

If you plan to evacuate

- Plan for personal safety and house safety modifications, as above.
- Prepare an evacuation plan and become familiar with all aspects. (See Chapter 20, Evacuate, defend or shelter?, 'Safe evacuation procedure' and Chapter 21, What to do when bushfire threatens, 'Early on day of bushfire danger')
- Read up on and think about every aspect of the evacuate–stay dilemma. (See The Complete Bushfire Safety Book, Chapter 12, The decision – evacuate or stay? Safety or suicide?)
  - ➤ Gain understanding of the factors that influence safe evacuation.
  - ➤ Gain understanding of how to work out when is 'early' enough for safe evacuation.
- Discuss ways of evacuating the family the day before or morning of a forecast bad day.

Realise:
- You could need to do this many times a season.
- Dangerous fires happen on days other than those with official warnings.
- Morning evacuation cannot assure safety.
  - ➢ An early arsonist could have lit a fire between your home and destination.
  - ➢ Fire can start at night from the flare-up of a previous fire.
  - ➢ Fire can be started in the afternoon or at night by lightning.
    - – In western Victoria, most lightning strikes occur in summer on January afternoons.
- There is seldom just 'a bushfire'.
  - ➢ Multiple fires can threaten from unknown localities.
- It is often not possible for an official warning to be given in time.
- Vacated houses are more likely to be destroyed.
- Though you may feel 'it doesn't matter about the house', it will matter afterwards.
- House replacement can prove difficult; crisis accommodation can be protracted.
- Large bushfire house losses seriously deplete the general housing supply.
- Find out whether there is a community shelter nearby.
- Check local community shelter regulations with municipal authority.
- Find out at what stage of bushfire threat it would become available to shelterers.
- Visit the shelter to ascertain whether it would actually be safer than your home.
  - ➢ Are there provisions for child care? Are pets allowed?
  - ➢ If shelter is open space, realise that you will be exposed to embers and firebrands.
    - – Obtain pure wool blankets for protection from these.
- If not satisfied, check whether a neighbour's house is better-protected than yours.
- Check the neighbour's willingness to shelter you.
- Ask friends in large towns or safe suburbs whether you could stay with them.
- Think about whether you could reach a refuge safely in bushfire conditions.
- Travel your proposed evacuation route.
  - ➢ Consider potential for fallen trees, extra traffic, traffic jams and smoke.
- Time trip to refuge both from home and work.
  - ➢ Allow extra time for bushfire conditions.
- Time how long it takes you to seal the house before you would leave it.
  - ➢ Windows closed, shutters down, inner and outer doors shut.
  - ➢ Grounds tidied.
  - ➢ Gutters filled with water.
- Time how long you would need to get everyone into protective clothing.
- Time how long it takes to load the car with people and pets.
- Time how long it takes to put stock in their safe refuge paddock before leaving.
- Prepare an emergency Plan B to shelter safely. (See Chapter 21, What to do when bushfire happens, 'Safe sheltering procedure')

Travel

- Check if planned holiday will be during the bushfire season for the areas to be visited.
- Check whether that district has a community bushfire refuge. (See Chapter 19, Protective travelling)
- Think about whether business trips will take you to potential bushfire areas.

Community planning

- Discuss creating parks with low-flammability trees on the fireward edge of town. (See Chapter 15, Township protection)
- Hold working bees to reduce the amount of fine fuel in and around your town.
- Discuss ways of sharing information and resources.
- Discuss plans to care for the less able-bodied people in your area.
- Develop network of phone contacts, 'phone-trees' and other warning systems.
  - ➢ Include mobile as well as landline numbers.
- Discuss benefits and deficiencies of any local community refuges.
- Form a community fireguard group.

People who choose to live in the bush must take the responsibility of planning and preparing for their own bushfire safety.
The rural fire brigade cannot possibly have a fire unit at every house.

15
Township protection

Reduction of in-town fuel is vital to township protection.
The amount of flammable vegetation *within* townships can exceed that in the bush.
Ember-throw from in-town ignitions can cause one-third of township losses.

Three options for residents of bushfire-prone towns

- Reduce the fuel load of adjacent forests to scientifically prescribed safe distances.
- Live with the annual fear of loss of life, home and livelihood.
- Move house, and live in an urban environment.

Three core activities to minimise township tragedies

- Reduce fuel around and within towns and around houses.
- Modify houses and other buildings to be impenetrable by flying embers.
- Teach residents how to react safely during a bushfire threat.

A systematically protected township can

- Survive any bushfire with most buildings intact.
- Survive with populations intact.

A haphazardly protected township can

- Be almost completely destroyed.
- Suffer much loss of life.

Township hazard increases with

- Proximity to bush that has dense undergrowth and highly flammable trees.
- Steep or rugged topography.
- Unreduced roadside vegetation.
- Cluttered private gardens.
- Flammable street planting.
- Small building blocks.
  - ➤ Especially those close to dense bush.
- Number of evacuated and undefended houses.

Township hazard decreases with

- Clearing of understorey and litter in adjacent bushland to appropriate distance.
- Reduction of flammable vegetation within township.
- Increased amount of fleshy plants and European deciduous trees in and around town.
- Sports grounds, parks, pools or low-flammability crops on the town's fireward sides.
- Less housing on sites of high bushfire hazard.
- Building blocks large enough to allow protective site and layout features.
- Wide roads around housing subdivisions.
- Roads interconnecting with others to avoid dead ends.
- Roads and bridges at least two lanes wide.
- Bridges built of non-flammable materials.

Tragedies would be dramatically reduced if applicants for building permits in bushfire-prone towns were required to pass a bushfire safety knowledge test – a 'licence to live there'.

Township protection plans require

1. Input from fire, council, horticultural and community representatives.
2. Fuel modification programs, outside the town and within it.
3. Modification of public buildings to bushfire-safe standards.
4. Schemes to increase community safety knowledge.
5. Schemes to assist residents to create safe properties.
6. Standards for safe gardens in bushfire-prone towns, as there are for buildings.
7. Optimum-standard community bushfire shelters.

1 Input from fire, council and community delegates

- Utilisation of local experience and expertise.
- Information exchange and understanding between township organisations.
- Utilisation of municipal resources to reduce fine fuel and debris within the town.
- Discussions with local public institutions to upgrade their bushfire safety.
  - ➢ Especially hospitals, hostels, schools and kindergartens.
- Plans for safety of aged and frail residents during bushfire emergencies.
- Planning for local early warning systems such as sirens or 'phone-trees'.
- Ways of sharing information and resources.
- Effective ways to disseminate information to residents.
- Regular information updates to residents.

> **Township protection has to take into account how flammable local vegetation is, for how long burning can persist in it and how far it can send embers.**

2 Fuel modification programs

- Awareness of potential fire speed and smoulder persistence of fuel in local bush.
- Reduction of highly flammable vegetation.
- Replacement with low-flammability plants.

In adjacent bush

- Prescribed burns to reduce fuel load hazard.
  - ➢ Can need from 300 m to 3 km. (See Chapter 7, A protective property layout)
  - ➢ Amount required varies with density and type of vegetation, and topography.
- Reduction of leaf litter to depth equivalent to very close-mown grass.
- Reduction of rough-barked trees where possible.
- Encouragement of smooth-barked, non-streamer forming trees.

Between town and bush

- Well-maintained fuelbreaks with vehicle access.
  - ➢ Could be graded trail, close-mown grass or annually burnt strip.

In parks and recreation areas

- Close-mown irrigated lawns and playing fields.
- No flammable mulch on garden beds.
- Replace with 75 mm deep compost, granitic sand, pebbles or road-metal crushings.
  - ➢ Ignited mulch pieces become embers that stay alight for than 30 minutes.
  - ➢ In Canberra 2003, masses of glowing mulch embers ignited other gardens and homes.
- Replacement of highly flammable plant species with species of low flammability.
  - ➢ Such as smooth-barked, bird-attracting box and red ironbarks.
- Predominance of deciduous trees with low summer leaf drop.
- Predominance of smooth-barked over rough-barked native trees.
- Removal of flammable conifers and rough-barked eucalypts.
- Reduced areas of flammable shrubs.
- Increased areas of fleshy plants.
- Paved, gravelled or stone areas near buildings. (See Chapter 8, A protective garden)

In private gardens

- Encouragement of all the recommendations made above in 'Parks and recreation areas'.
- Summer campaigns to clear backyards of building materials, tyres, old cars.

Around public buildings

- Encouragement of all the recommendations made above in 'Parks and recreation areas'.

On farms and plantations

- Maintenance of heavily grazed pastures on north and west sides.
- Bare-earth fuelbreaks around house, sheds, fences and haystacks.
- Wood piles and timber stacks on south or east sides.
- Fuel reduction within native wood-lots.
- Pruning of conifer (pine) wood-lots to 8 m from the ground.
  - ➢ Pruning to 6 m did not prevent crown fires in *Pinus radiata* in Canberra, 2003.
- Removal of surface pine needles, branch and log debris.

On roadsides both out of, and within, town

- Maintenance by mowing.
- Encouragement of low-flammability shrubs.

Roadside plantings of native vegetation by environmental groups restricted to

- Least flammable species.
  - ➢ Smooth-trunked trees that don't shed bark during the bushfire season.
- Space between individual trees.
- Clumps of vegetation isolated from other clumps.
- Plantings well away from housing.

The more fuel reduction in the bush, the less embers enter the town.
Low-hazard vegetation may need reduction for 300 m into the bush.
High-hazard vegetation may need reduction for up to 3 km from town.

---

3 Modification of public buildings

- Features to discourage ember entry.
  - ➢ Roll-down metal shutters on windows and external doors.
  - ➢ Mesh covers on air conditioning units.
- Features to discourage cladding ignition.
  - ➢ Modification of vegetation types and planting design.
  - ➢ Low-flow roof sprinkler systems. (See Chapter 9, A protective house design)
- Schools, kindergartens, hospitals and business premises need similar attention.

4 Schemes to increase community safety knowledge

- Bushfire safety teaching in schools.
- Bushfire safety workshops in factories, businesses, hospitals.
- Teachers, hospital and venue CEOs to learn, practise and pass on safe procedures.
  - ➢ Only by saturating towns with knowledge will it enter the national psyche.

5 Schemes to assist residents to create safe properties

- Active and well-practised resident groups such as Community Fireguard.
- Grants or low-interest loans to low-income residents to make their properties safer.
- Assistance to help less able residents put their properties in a safe state.
- Penalties for residents whose persistently neglected properties endanger neighbours.
- Refusal of building permits for blocks in, or adjacent to, dense bushland.
  - ➢ Unless applicant can demonstrate competence in bushfire-safe maintenance.

6 Standards for safe gardens in bushfire-prone areas

- Trees cleared of shrubs, long grass and debris beneath their canopies.
- Branches pruned to well above the ground, and from walls and roof.
- Pine trees' lower branches pruned to 8 m.
- Dead bark removed from forks in trees.
- Trees and shrubs set out singly, or in clumps separated from each other.
- Native trees and pines distanced 50 m from the house.
- European deciduous trees.
  - ➤ Especially on the firewind side of houses.
- Thick- and smooth-, rather than rough-barked trees.
- Fleshy and other low-flammability plants.
- Grass kept short and, if possible, well-watered.
- Leaves and litter raked from around the house.
- Non-flammable mulches: no pine bark, woodchips, straw, sawdust, dung pats.
- No shrubs against windows.
- Paths between garden beds and flammable walls.
- Firewood stacked well away from house and trees.
- Non-flammable fences.
- Non-flammable outdoor furniture.
- Overhead sprinkler system
- Radiant heat shields.
- Nature strip mown, grazed, gravelled or paved.

**A big problem with relying on any shelter away from home is how to get there safely.
Travel to a bushfire refuge should never be acted on as a 'last resort'.
A decision to seek refuge away from home must be a pre-planned bushfire response.**

---

7 Optimum-standard community bushfire shelters

- Multiplicity, so that outlying evacuees can safely and quickly reach one.
  - ➤ A central situation within a built-up township is of limited use to outer residents.
- Types of shelter (building, open space) suited to degree of local risk.
- Well-marked, short routes that are safe for travel in bushfire conditions.
  - ➤ A huge danger of such refuges is travel to them by outlying evacuees.
- Solid building with protected windows and doors, secure roof and sheltered exits.
  - ➤ Metal roll-down window and door shutters
  or
  - ➤ fire-rated solid-core door with metal mesh screen and draught-stoppers.

- Roof structurally strong enough to withstand winds over 150 km/h.
- Roof secured with cyclone clips.
- Mesh covers over skylights and external air conditioner units.
- Clear of flammable vegetation for at least 40 m.
- Entirely clear of woodchip mulch.
- Non-flammable furnishings and wall linings that do not emit toxic gases if alight.
- Ventilation that does not admit smoke.
- Roof and ground sprinklers.
- Large reserve water supply, independent of mains pressure.
- Space to accommodate local evacuees plus tourists.
- Access early on each day of announced bushfire danger, and for its duration.
- Facilities for water, food and rest.
- Amenities for babies and the frail.
- Shade and water for pets.
- Provision of fire-safe blankets (preferably pure wool) for last-resort protection.
- Sufficient toilets.
- First aid and firefighting equipment.
- Sufficient parking, clear of flammable trees, grass, woodchips, buildings.
- Facility for dual-purpose venues to convert from normal activities at short notice.
- Those who work in dual-purpose venues to understand their emergency purpose.
- The emergency purpose of seldom-used community refuges to be frequently maintained.
- Public recognition that:
  - ➢ The houses vacated by shelterers will have a high incidence of unimpeded ignition.

Some safety can be provided by

- Tunnels.
- Brick toilet blocks.

Questionable safety can be provided by

- Open spaces such as sports grounds, parks, race tracks and beaches.
  - ➢ Disadvantage of exposure to heat, smoke, embers and firebrands.
  - ➢ Must have no adjacent flammable vegetation.

> The 2009 Royal Commission's concept of Neighbourhood Safer Places
> as community bushfire shelters is fundamentally flawed.
> The Commission warns people who consider using a Neighbourhood Safer Place
> to be aware of their limitations.

Neighbourhood Safer Places (NSPs)[1]

- Though titled 'Safer Places', their definition declares 'they cannot be considered safe'.
- They can be open spaces with no shelter from falling embers, firebrands or smoke.
- They will not be available for early, precautionary evacuation.
- Many aspects contravene accepted bushfire authority safety advice.
- They are specified as 'places of last resort', to go to 'during the passage of a fire'.
  - ➢ Travel while fire is in the area is potentially perilous.
- Safe access during bushfire conditions is not a requirement for NSPs.
- They are not for all-day or night-time use.
- They will not be staffed.
- They need have no amenities – even water.
- They do not cater for animals.
- They need not have features that offer more safety than a well-prepared house.

> The safest 'shelter of last resort' is a pure wool blanket.

---

1   *Royal Commission Interim Report No 1. par 8.26,* and *NSP-assessment-guidelines-1* (CFA 2010)
    http://www.saferplaces.cfa.vic.gov.au/cfa/search/default.htm

16
Protective chores

Protective chores

Around the house

- Make and mend, paint and fill.
  - ➤ Aim – to prevent bushfire embers entering the house.

Around the grounds

- Slash, mow, rake, prune, tidy, burn, water.
  - ➤ Aim – to lower the intensity of a bushfire by reducing vegetation.
  - ➤ And therefore reduce embers, flame reach and radiant heat.

House chore checklist

Protective features you may need to install

- Window shutters.
- Metal mesh coverings over doors, windows, vents, cracks, chimneys.
- Fire-rated external doors.
- Better latches on doors if they do not stay closed during strong wind.
- Weather seals to external doors.
- Draught-stoppers to external doors.
- Insulation to wall cavity, subfloor and ceiling space.
- Low flow roof sprinklers. Leaf-free guttering.

Winter and spring chores

Timber cladding and window ledges

- Affix non-combustible materials to return corners of flammable cladding.
- Inspect for peeling paint, cracks, patches of rot in which sparks could lodge.
- Sand down rough patches.
- Fill cracks with expandable low-flammability sealant.
- Sand smooth again.
- Paint any treated pine posts that are part of the house structure.
  - ➢ Smouldering treated pine emits toxic gas.

Subfloor

- Enclose gap-boards or open subfloor with 1 m high non-flammable material.
- Clear of vegetation and litter.

Verandah or deck timber floors

- Replace loose or rotted boards.
- Coat with a smooth, non-resinous, low-flammability finish.
- Install metal sheeting where timber floors and steps abut house wall.
- Cover gapped timber decking boards with metal flywire.

Roof

- Eliminate or protect angled roof junctions. (See Chapter 9, A protective house design)
- Cover skylights, ventilators, air conditioner intakes with metal mesh covers.
- Secure loose tiles, sheets and ridge capping. Install low flow sprinklers.
- Fill nail holes in galvanised iron roofing.
- Check and repair roof insulation.
- Clear spouting of accumulated leaves.
- Repair rusted areas of gutters.
  - ➢ So that gutters retain water when bushfire threatens.

Ceiling space

- Clear out stored goods, papers, rubbish, birds', rats' or possums' nests.
- Make as dust-free as possible.
  - ➢ Commercial contractors will vacuum ceiling space.
- Insulate above and below rafters.
- If you don't have an inspection trapdoor, make one.
  - ➢ These are vital bushfire-protection chores.

> **Because it is not easily observed, the ceiling space is very vulnerable.
> Ignition in the ceiling space
> is a major cause of house destruction and of the deaths of shelterers.**

Chimneys and flues

- Clean.
- Install or repair metal flywire covers.
  - ➤ A sooty chimney can send sparks flying over the countryside.

Eaves, fascias and fluted roof edging

- Check for cracks.
- Fill and sand smooth.

Windows

- Install roll-down metal shutters.
  - ➤ Manual inside operation is needed, as electricity often fails during a bushfire.
- Check that they operate easily and close securely.
  - ➤ You may need the manufacturer or agent to maintain them.
- Make emergency covers. (See Chapter 9, A protective house design)
- Check that outer mesh screens have no holes.

Pergolas

- Cover fibreglass roof or creeper with metal mesh.

LP gas bottles

- Turn relief valve away from wall. Check this frequently.
- Check for cracks and other weaknesses.
  - ➤ Intact gas bottles are unlikely to explode during a bushfire.
- Check that they are securely fixed in place.
- Enclose in metal mesh.
  - ➤ Metal mesh allows leaking gas to escape without danger of explosion.
- Set on a concrete base and fix securely to a strong metal pipe.
- If possible, site at least 6 m from house in a cleared area 6 m diameter.
- Never lie an LPG cylinder on its side.
  - ➤ If heat causes the liquid gas inside it to boil and be unable to escape, it will explode.

Timber fences

- Check for rotted crossbeams, and repair.
  - ➤ These are ember traps.
- Strap loose fence posts to crossbeams with galvanised metal strips.
- Strip any oiled fences. Paint over if necessary.
  - ➤ Oiled timber fences feed fire.

Timber fence posts on farms

- Replace with metal drops.
  - ➤ If even every second post is metal, the wire will be held if timber posts burn.

Gates

- Repaint if needed.
- Repair hinges so they can be easily opened during a fire emergency.

Sheds and garages

- Tidy them.
  - ➤ You must be able to easily get at and douse any entering embers.
- Install shutters or metal mesh over windows or replace with wired glass.
- Put oily rags and other flammables into closed metal containers.

A house declared *undefendable* can be made defendable through care with chores.
And a house declared *defendable* can become undefendable through neglect of chores.

Mid-spring or early summer chores – *elevated fire danger*

Personal protection

- Check whether anyone has grown out of last summer's protective clothing.
- Check that items are in good condition.
- Discuss whether more pure wool blankets are needed.

Precious possessions

- Prepare a safe 'bunker' for them, take to a suburban friend or put them in storage.

Timber window frames

- Check for secure closure after they've dried out from winter dampness.

Firefighting facilities

- Check for working effectiveness. Repair or replace if necessary.
  - ➢ Pumps may need to be sent to the manufacturer for checking.
- If hoses leak, cut out the part with the hole and rejoin.
- Check that knapsack spray pumps, sprayers are working.
  - ➢ Keep filled during the bushfire season.

Discuss your preparations with neighbours.
Join or start a community fireguard group.

Garden and farm chore checklist

Winter chores

Vegetation management

- Remove rough-, loose-barked and large eucalypts to 50 m from house.
  - ➢ Accumulated leaf and litter on extremely dry, windy days can endanger your house.
- Remove conifers, including ornamental pencil pines, to 50 m from house.
  - ➢ These burn ferociously.
- Remove *Pinus radiata* or prune lower branches to 8 m from the ground.
- Weed out flammable plants or space from each other and from buildings.
  - ➢ A suitable distance apart for the separation of eucalypts is 7 m.

Spring chores

Vegetation management

(See Chapter 8, A Protective garden)
- Inspect the garden for clutter and flammability.
- Remodel continuous garden beds into separated areas.

- Remove woodchip mulch or cover with earth or pebbles.
  - ➢ Burning mulch causes huge house losses. Embers can stay alight for 30 minutes.
  - ➢ Non-flammable mulches are compost, granitic sand and pebbles.
- Transplant shrubs away from walls and windows.
- Remove vines from flammable walls and pergolas or cover with metal mesh.
- Put metal mesh over fibreglass pergolas.
- Create paths between garden beds and windows or flammable walls.
- Start planting low-flammability trees and shrubs.
- Prune remaining smooth-barked trees for 2 m from walls and ground.
- Plant the trees that will form windbreak hedges.
- Check whether existing hedges and shrubs are green and alive right through.
- Strip messy bark from trees beyond the 50 m zone.
  - ➢ Some bark can stay alight, airborne, for 30 km.
- Move woodheaps from verandahs, against flammable walls, and beneath trees.

Water supply
- Check that reserve tanks are full.
- Buy in water to fill them if necessary.
- Check and reinforce tank rivets and solder where needed.
- Clear the access outlets of reticulated water pipes.
- Clear sprinkler system spray nozzles that may have become clogged.
- Check condition of hoses and number of hose connections.
  - ➢ Aim to have enough hoses to wet any part of house, garden or fence.

Early summer chores – *elevated fire danger*

Vegetation management
- Clear and clean up.
  - ➢ Around buildings, tank, machinery, fuels, stockyards, beneath trees.
  - ➢ Get rid of derelict vehicles, broken toys, boxes and other rubbish.
- Clear gutters of leaves.
- Cover plastic weedmats with pebbles, earth or mulch.
- Move plastic pots away from walls or transfer plants to terracotta pots.
  - ➢ Plastic pots are flammable.
- Dig shallow ditches to catch blowing, burning leaves and litter.

Firefighting equipment

Repeat checks made in mid-spring, as above, plus:

- Gather a collection of water containers and water dispensers.
  - ➤ Old baths, drums, barrels, buckets.
  - ➤ Knapsacks, stirrup pumps, garden sprayers, water guns, mops, jugs, dippers.
- Fill and place them around all buildings now, especially near core areas.
  - ➤ Have them there, ready, all through summer.

**The more preparation you do now,
the less there is to do on a day of fire danger.**

Whole of summer chores

Electronic equipment

- Keep computer backed up and mobile phone charged.
- Keep important computer files on memory stick worn round your neck or on keyring.

Vegetation management

- Keep gutters, roof valleys and around buildings clear of leaves.
  - ➤ A single windy summer's day can drop 2 t/ha in gutters and on grounds.
- Clear long grass and litter.
  - ➤ For 20 m from buildings, plus 1 m for each degree of slope.
  - ➤ From under house, water tank stands, around incinerators and woodheaps.
  - ➤ Between and under buildings, shrubs and trees. Outside fences.
- Keep grass near house cut short and well-watered if possible.
- Mow grass very short for 20 m from crops and 10 m from buildings.
- Rake away all mowed vegetation.
  - ➤ Don't leave lying in heaps – compost, burn, use as hay, bin or take to tip.
  - ➤ Rotting cut grass ignites more easily from embers than does standing dead grass.
- Slash where mower can't reach – under trees, along fences, around buildings.
  - ➤ Clear away slashed vegetation.
- Re-slash as it re-grows.
  - ➤ May need to be done in patches to safeguard native animals' habitat/food.
- If using mechanical slasher, watch slashings for signs of smouldering from sparks.

- Rake under trees, around buildings, woodheaps, in barns.
  - ➢ Bits of paper, rags, woodchips and dead weeds act as fire starters for embers.
- Get rid of the rakings.
- Thin undergrowth and litter in adjacent bush.
- Remove loose bark and dead branches from trees.
- Weed self-seeded saplings as they come up.
- Weed orchards between rows and under trees.
- Clear litter from access tracks through paddocks and at creek crossings.

Water use (when watering restrictions permit)

- Lawns each day.
- Established shrubs twice a week.
- Established introduced trees once or twice a week (deep-watered).
  - ➢ If leaves are falling, give longer watering.
  - ➢ Well-hydrated trees have not burned even in the most intense fire situations.
- Established trees indigenous to the area rarely need watering.

Farm vehicles and machinery chore checklist

- Regularly lubricate pumps, chainsaws and slashers so bearings won't overheat.
- Keep spark arresters clean and in good order.
- Check manifolds, mufflers, tail pipes and fuel lines for leaks.
- Check stone guards, bash plates and exhaust systems for entangled dry grass.
- Keep machinery cleaned of oil and grease.
- Where there are engines near haystacks, keep exhaust pointed away from hay.

When operating machinery

- Carry a knapsack spray pump.
- If near vegetation, check often behind you for fire.
- When welding, keep 1.5 m around cleared of flammables and wetted down.

Power lines

- Inspect frequently to see that branches have not fouled them.
- Prune trees away from power lines for a distance equal to the tree's mature height.
- Prune shrubs to 10 m from poles and 3 m from lines.
- Check pole stability by banging with the back of an axe.
  - ➢ Solid wood makes a sound different from rotted wood.

Fuel tanks

- Each day, check for leaks and ensure bungs fit tightly.
- Check valves for blockages.
- Frequently rake ground around fuel stands.

Late summer–autumn chores

Haystacks

- For three months after a stack is built, check its temperature daily.
  - ➤ Maintain at less than 71°C, to avoid spontaneous internal combustion.
- Make sure the stack has gaps.
- In shedded stacks, check for space between hay and side walls.
- Repair walls if they could catch sparks.
- Keep fuelbreaks cleared for 20 m all around.
- Do not burn off around haystacks – plough, graze, mow or use weedkiller.

Your bushfire safety can be in your own hands – and in your hoes.

Fuelbreaks chore checklist

Autumn to mid-winter

- Prepare fallows for stock refuges and fuelbreaks.
  - ➤ Start before grass begins to grow strongly.

Late winter

- Graze fuelbreaks and stock refuges at twice the normal rate.
- Graze stock along roadsides, using temporary fences.
- Tether a grazing pet in different areas to systematically close-crop whole area.

Early spring

- Intensify grazing near house, sheds, laneways and paddocks.
- Sow low-flammability summer crops.

Late spring – *elevated fire danger*

- Re-cultivate fuelbreaks.
- Work fallow areas over again.
  - ➤ How often this chore needs repeating depends on the vigour of grass growth.
- Start controlled burning. (See Chapter 17, Safe burn-offs)
- Graze fuelbreaks and stock refuges at five times the normal rate.

Stock refuges chore checklist

Autumn to mid-winter

- Prepare fallows.

Late winter

- Graze at twice the normal rate.

Spring

- Graze at five times the normal rate.
  - ➤ Ground should then be bare by summer.
- Plant low-flammability shade trees and windbreaks.
- Create fuelbreaks.

From early summer

- Check stock drinking water supply.

Throughout the year

Weather watching

- Study local weather and try to relate it to bushfire conditions.
- Become familiar with local variations of the wind.
- Note where leaves and twigs land when they blow over your house.
- Note how clouds, sunsets and sunrises relate to local weather changes.
- Consult media and internet each day for bushfire weather trends.

- Be aware that media maps and internet postings can be hours out of date.
  - ➤ The weather pattern may well have moved on from this.
- Keep a bushfire weather danger record for your district.
- On days of fire danger, watch the actual weather around you.

Family bushfire drill

- Practise your defending, evacuating or sheltering plans at least once a month.
  - ➤ Wearing protective clothing.

**What is needed even more than well-prepared houses
is well-prepared people.**

17
Safe burn-offs

The aim is for a gentle fire that creeps about.

Standard of a good burn-off

- Removes litter and low shrubs but does not scorch leaves of trees.
  - ➢ Scorch height is three to five times flame height.

A good day to burn off

- Temperature 20°C or less.
  - ➢ The hotter the air, the drier the vegetation, the faster it ignites and flames move.
- Wind 20 km/h or less.
  - ➢ At 10 km/h leaves rustle, at 20 km/h small twigs move.
- Relative humidity 40–60%.
- Time after 10 a.m.
  - ➢ Early morning stillness often changes.

Conditions for a good burn-off

- In bushland – when ground litter is dry enough to burn properly.
- In grassland – when grass is cured.

The paperwork

- Check permit requirements with local authority.
- Obtain weather forecast and fire danger rating.

- Prepare a burning plan.
  - ➤ What, when, what with and what to do if burn escapes. (See below)
- Notify and discuss with neighbours.
- Make signs to put out for travellers.

Burning off is tricky:
fire can escape to cause a dangerous bushfire.
A great number of factors must be taken into account.

Preparation

- Clear 2 m between intended burn area and fences or buildings.
- Slash and clear away grass from beneath trees.
- Make firebreaks around the area to be burnt.

You will need

- Easily accessible and plentiful water.
- 18–30 L knapsack sprays.
- Hoses, rakes, sprayers, rakehoes and beaters.
- Protective clothing and smoke masks.
- Enough helpers and equipment to keep the burn within fuelbreaks.

Plan for a safe burn-off

- Burn against the wind and downhill.
- Burn well-spaced small spots of fire in a series of strips.
- Start next strip only after the previous one is completely burnt and black.

Safety rules for burn-offs

- Never leave a burn-off unattended.
- Never burn off alone. Always arrange help.
  - ➤ You need people to patrol boundaries and deal with escapes of fire.
- Wear protective clothing, mask and goggles.

- Have a pure wool blanket, foil tent or throw-over for emergency shelter.
- If flames grow higher than 1 m, put the fire out.
- If the burn becomes hard to control, call the fire service at once.
- Patrol and mop up until fire is out and cold.
- Check again next morning.

(For more comprehensive information see *The Complete Bushfire Safety Book*, Chapter 11, How to prepare for bushfire season)

The burning of a grass stalk can be over in two seconds, so grass burn-offs are extremely sensitive to wind fluctuations.

How to suppress a fire

- Carry tools at the hip.
- Wear gloves for handling burning logs.
- Pour water on the burning fuel, not the flames

  or
- cover burning fuel with water or earth

  or
- beat burning fuel with green leaves or wet bag or mop.
  - ➤ Do not beat burning, rough-barked trees.
- Rake sparks *towards* burning fuel.
- Remove unburnt vegetation and litter from the path of a fire.
- Do not stamp out flames.
  - ➤ People have died from ignited trousers.
- Shield yourself from radiant heat.
- Shelter eyes with wetted arm, keep eyelids half-closed.
- Drink from the hose and wet yourself with it.
- Do not stand in dense vegetation.
- Keep near an escape route to bare or burnt ground.
- Do not let yourself become overtired.
  - ➤ If you feel overfatigued, weak or dizzy, move to a safe area.
- Take care not to trip.
- If clothes catch fire, roll on the ground.
- Be meticulous in mopping up.
- Do not use water on gas, petrol, kerosene or grease fires.

If trapped by flames

- Turn hose or knapsack on yourself.
- Cover yourself with pure wool blanket or aluminium foil tent.
- Move downhill towards side and rear of fire, but only if a clear route is accessible.
- Do not run uphill.
- Do not try to escape along a gully.
  - ➤ Gullies speed up fire as it is funnelled through.
- Do not go through flames more than calf height or 1.5 m deep.

Where to shelter if trapped by flames

- On burnt or bare ground.
- In culvert, dugout, tunnel, dam, river, cave, ditch, wombat hole or wheel ruts.
- Behind rocks or large tree trunk.
  - ➤ Clear vegetation from near shelter.

How to shelter if trapped by flames

- Cover yourself with earth, pure wool blanket or thick coat.
- Lie down.
- Cover your nose.
- Limit breathing rate.
- Breathe fresh pockets of air low to ground.
- Do not shelter in a watertank.
  - ➤ Immersion in heated water rapidly increases core body temperature.
  - ➤ When this exceeds 42°C, a person becomes incapacitated and can drown.

Go through flames only if

- There is a clear area no further than two or three steps away on the other side.
- You can see over the top of the flames.
- Your shoes will protect both tops and soles of feet.
- You have covered all exposed body parts including hands, face and head.

**Escapes from badly managed burn-offs
is the greatest single cause of bushfires.**

18

Protecting domestic animals, stock and sanctuaries

> Be aware that your pet may not be allowed to accompany you
> on community evacuation transport or to a community bushfire refuge.
> And that boarding facilities may not have vacancies if bushfire happens during holidays.

Animals and bushfire

- Small animals are quickly affected by heat and by smoke inhalation.
- Caged birds and pigs can die from heat stress.
- Sheep suffer more bushfire injuries than cattle and horses.
  - ➢ Sheep run and pack against paddock fences, so that those on the edge get burnt.
  - ➢ Cattle and horses escape more easily through fence openings.
- Dogs and cats burnt on the feet and face can recover with veterinary treatment.
- Horses sustain serious hoof injuries if their metal shoes contact hot surfaces.
- Native animals normally escape from mild bushfires.

Planning ahead

- Ask local council and animal welfare bodies about emergency support plans.
- Update identity tags and/or microchip to ensure that lost pets can be returned.
  - ➢ Check that your current *mobile* number is on tag or registration database.
- Note your veterinarian's contact details on collar or tag.
- Have a recent photograph available.

- Arrange with friends in a low-risk area to mind pets on risky days
  or
- for permission to take pets to work.
  - ➢ As with children and the frail, transport pets the evening before the risk.
- Update pets' vaccinations and have proof of it available.
  - ➢ Boarding facilities and emergency centres usually require this.
- Pack a pet survival kit. (See below)

Tips for safe pets

If staying with your house

- Take pets into the house with you.
- Keep collars on dogs all through a high-risk day, and leashes handy.
  - ➢ For easy restraint if they take fright at strong wind or other noises.
- Have cat cages prepared.
- Keep pets cool.
- Keep them comforted and reassured.
- Give them water.

If evacuating

- Take dogs and small caged animals with you if not already accommodated.
- Take plenty of drinking water for them.
  - ➢ In heat-resistant containers.
- Put collars on dogs and attach leashes before exiting the house.
  - ➢ Fear can make them try to run away before you get them to the car.
- Place cats in a boarding cattery or veterinary clinic.
  - ➢ Keeping cats contained and comfortable in a carry-cage for long is difficult.
  - ➢ The emergency accommodation must not be vulnerable to bushfire.
  Or
- if allowable, take your pets to work with you.
- Notify someone whether you have taken your animals with you or left them.
- Inform where animals have been left – at home or in accommodation.
- If evacuating a valuable animal, plan appropriate transport and all it needs.
- Carry out such evacuations early, preferably the day before expected risk.
  - ➢ Smoke may panic a horse, make it difficult to load or cause it injure itself.
- Be aware that your own emergency accommodation may be long-term.

> **Attempts to hastily evacuate horses by float as fire approaches
> are more likely to end in disaster and death than in escape – for you and them.**

Pet survival kits

- Pure wool or leather coat for dogs.
- Pure wool cover for bird cages and cat cages.
- Collar and lead/halter for each animal.
- Bedding or rugs.
- Food, water and containers.
- Medications.
- Vaccination cards and medical records.
- Favourite toys.
- Grooming aids.
- Litter trays and litter for cats.
- Temporary fencing for livestock that are to be moved.
  - ➢ Battery-powered electric fence unit, electric tape, tread-ins or star pickets.

Home-based refuges for animals

Refuges for dogs

- Bare ground 3 m around kennel.
- Kennel protected by European deciduous trees.
- Low wall or low-flammability shrubs 2 m to fireward of kennel to shield three sides.
  - ➢ Do not entirely fence, cage or tether dog.
- Kennel constructed of non-flammable materials.
  - ➢ Particularly the roof.
- Earth mounds or ditches on firewind sides of kennel to halt rolling embers.
- Drinking water in heat-resistant container that will not blow away.

Refuges for fowl pens and aviaries

- Sprinklers for roof and walls.
- Low wall 2–3 m to fireward of pen to shield three sides.
- Protected by European deciduous trees.
  - ➢ Cover small aviary with pure wool blanket or strong foil if embers fall.

Refuges for horses

- Stables of brick, stone or concrete.
  - ➢ Roof and perimeter sprinklers.
  - ➢ Cleared 10 m around.
  - ➢ Remove straw, soak timber doors, fill water troughs.
- In paddock – bare earth beneath a large, spreading, low-flammability shade tree.
  - ➢ 20–30 m bare if there are other trees in the paddock.
  - ➢ 10 m bare if only grass in the paddock.
  - ➢ Water trough, filled daily.
  - ➢ Radiant heat shield wall or hedge, 4 m long and at least as high as the horse.

If agisted

- Arrange for the landowner to refuge or release your horse on word from you
  or
- collect your horse on a bad fire-danger day, early in the morning.
  - ➢ Tether it in shade near your house.
  - ➢ Where suitable, take it into easily accessed small room such as a laundry.
  - ➢ Cover its back and head with pure wool blanket.
  - ➢ Cover its face with a cloth to prevent panic.

In all cases where horses are not being evacuated

- ➢ Remove metal shoes.
- ➢ Remove rugs, fly-veils, halters – plastic can melt and metal buckles burn flesh.

Never leave any domestic animal tethered or caged outside during bushfire.

Refuges for stock

- Can save farmers crippling re-stocking costs.
- Can save years of heartache for pet owners.
- Can prevent terrible suffering for hundreds of thousands of animals. (See Chapter 16, Protective chores, 'Stock refuges chore checklist')

Stock refuge layout

- On leeward side of the property.
- In the inner zone of protection. (See Chapter 7, A protective property layout)

Stock refuges need

- Fuelbreaks at least 6 m wide on the usual firewind sides.
- Hedges as wind/firebreak/radiation shields on at least two windward sides.
- Water in heat-resistant containers.
- Shade.
- Enough space to hold all stock.

Stock refuge suggestions

- Ploughed land.
- Well eaten-out paddock.
- Paddock planted with a green summer crop.
- Concrete milking sheds or stables.
- A nearby green, sheltered, open space such as golf links or recreation grounds.
- Heavily grazed lanes, not tree-lined.
- Dams with soil scooped up on at least two windward sides.
- Strongly gated trench 3 m deep into which cattle have been trained to move.

Stock refuge tips

- Clear straw and other flammables from milking sheds or stables.
- Clear flammable vegetation from earth mounds and trench rims.
- Fit property with internal gates that can be opened for animals to move to safety.

Protection for wildlife sanctuaries and pet resorts

- Sprinklers attached to perimeter fences and placed throughout grounds.
- Predominance of smooth-barked trees where suitable for habitat.
- Bushes and other fine fuel vegetation separate from trees.
- Bare ground, dam or creek available, if possible, for emergency animal retreat.

**Farm animals with severe burns often recover
if given intensive veterinary care and good nursing.**

19
Protective travelling

A car is a safe refuge in a grass fire.
It can be a safe refuge in a mild fire.
It is seldom a safe refuge in an intense forest fire.

Bushfire season data

- The start and duration of the bushfire season varies throughout Australia.
- The farther north you travel, the earlier in the year the bushfire season starts.
- The farther south you travel, the later the bushfire season starts.
  - ➤ The differences are caused by regional climate and season, particularly dry weather.

Regional bushfire seasons

- Northern Territory (northern regions): June–December.
- Queensland (southern regions): September–December.
- Queensland (western regions): September–February.
- New South Wales: October–February.
- Northern Territory (southern regions): October–March.
- Victoria: October–April.
- Western Australia (northern regions): October–November
- Tasmania: November–March.
- South Australia: November–April.
- Australian Capital Territory: December–March.
- Western Australia: (southern regions): February–March.
  (For fuller details see *The Complete Bushfire Safety Book*, Chapter 2, Bushfire cycles –'Bushfire weather')

Before you travel

- Check whether you will be travelling in a region's bushfire season.
- Check route for bushfire hazardous countryside – Google a map.
- Phone or email municipal offices of towns en route and ask about community refuges.
- Obtain protective equipment.
    - Fire extinguisher, knapsack, garden sprayer.
    - Pure wool blankets for passenger protection.
    - Fire-protective cover for car and trailer.
    - Rakehoe for emergency vegetation clearing.
    - Battery-operated radio or CB, mobile phone.
- Prepare survival kit for each traveller. (See Chapter 12, Protective equipment)
    - Pack them in an easily accessible place.
- Put a copy of *Essential Bushfire Safety Tips* in glovebox.
- Service the car.

On the road

- Do not travel into an area of potential bushfire danger on fire danger days.
    - Even major highways can be cut off by fire and you can be trapped.
    - Learn the ember-flinging potential of forests and grass fires.
- Listen to radio or CB on a bushfire warning channel throughout your journey.
- Never drive on narrow, bushy roads when there is any possibility of bushfire in the area.
- Do not drive towards a location where you can see smoke.
    - A bushfire could be heading towards you.
- Do not drive through smoke.
- If you see smoke ahead or smell it, turn back to a safe place.
    - Report quickly any fires you see.
- Have children watch for roadside bare areas that could be used in emergency.
- Keep water bottles topped up.

You can survive in a car provided the car does not catch alight.
If it does, you can survive if it can protect you until the fire outside has died down.

Is the car a safe refuge?

- Cars can be death traps in most forest fires.
- Cars are suitable shelters only:
  - ➢ In grass fires or very mild forest fires.
  - ➢ In areas well clear of fuel and distanced from radiant heat or flames.
- People who have died in cars during bushfires have usually:
  - ➢ Driven in smoke and crashed.
  - ➢ Driven into burning bushland.
  - ➢ Driven from burning bushland into an unburnt area that then ignited.
  - ➢ Been trapped by fire developed from embers that spotted ahead of or beside them.
  - ➢ Parked beside, on or under flammable vegetation.
  - ➢ Driven through flames.
  - ➢ Driven with windows down, allowing embers to ignite the interior of the car.

Car refuge safety depends on

- Fire intensity, flame height and amount of vegetation.
- Distance of car from flames.
- The duration of flames.
  - ➢ Grass fire flames last five to 15 seconds. You can exit safely onto scorched ground.
  - ➢ Forest fire flames can last five minutes. Cars can ignite before it is safe to exit.
  - ➢ Fire persisting in heavy fuel on roadsides can prevent you escaping to burnt ground.
  - ➢ Heat can be lethal for an hour after forest flames subside, if not protectively clothed.
- Size of clearing.
  - ➢ At least a 10 m circle of bare earth around the car and 10 m clear above ground.
  - ➢ If space is large enough and properly cleared, fire can go over and around car.
- Height and forward slope of flames.
  - ➢ Intense forest fires can have flames twice tree height.
  - ➢ Radiant heat from these kill even in a 10 m clearing.
- Condition of car.

As with houses, cars burn down from the inside.
When people die in cars they are killed by the fuel *inside* the car:
fibreglass, hydraulic fluids, petrol, plastic linings and insulation.

Car danger data

- Duco burns in 15 seconds when car is 4.5 m from 3 m high flames leaning at a 40° angle.
- Upholstery and trims can burn within one minute.
- After the duco flashes over, tyres ignite, windows shatter and fuel lines rupture.
- Fire erupts in the engine compartment, burns under the car and linings ignite.
- Disintegrating linings emit flammable gases.
- Molten plastic covers occupants.
- Unbearable pain from hot fittings on bare skin can force shelterers out of cars.
- Utility trucks ignite more easily than sedans.
  - ➤ Material in their trays can be ignited by embers.
- People who flee from unbearably hot cars during forest fires rarely survive.

Suitable pull-up shelter places

- Roadside verge clear of vegetation.
  - ➤ Except for wide-spreading European deciduous trees, which have low ignition risk.
- Wayside stop.
- Brick or other masonry toilet blocks.
- Dam or river.
  - ➤ Pull-up area must be cleared of flammable vegetation.
- Close under a cliff *above which* a fire is approaching.
  - ➤ The fire will jump over you.
- Sports ground, picnic ground, golf course, school ground.
  - ➤ Not under flammable trees or on grass.
- Beach.
- Rocky ground.
- In a quarry.
- Fallow paddock.
- Wide driveway.

**Many travellers who have died when confronted by grass fires
would almost certainly have survived had they stayed in their cars.**

How to take refuge in the car

- Park on bare ground cleared for at least 10 m around and above the car.
- If possible, place the car in a position that will avoid large embers and fierce heat.
- Close windows and vents.
- Put on your protective clothing.
- Spread protective cream or even mud on face and hands.
- Cover nose with mask or scarf. Put on goggles.
- Rake litter from under the car and around it for 10 m.
- Scatter raked fuel well away downwind.
- Park the car facing into the wind.
    - ➤ If the fuel tank ignites, its flames will blow away from you.
- Turn off the engine.
    - ➤ Cars stall very easily in bushfire heat due to vapourisation at carburettor.
    - ➤ Leaving the engine running will not necessarily prevent this.
- Cover pack-rack and trailer with non-flammable cover.
- Cover seats with pure wool blankets, to minimise burns from over-hot upholstery.
- Turn headlights on.
    - ➤ Other drivers are more likely to see you in the smoke and less likely to crash into you.
- When embers fall thickly or flames arrive, get into the car.
- Cover people and pets with blankets.
- Turn air conditioner to recirculate. Not to 'intake', as this draws in smoke.
    - ➤ In a mild fire, this could keep the inside of the car below lethal temperature.
- Erect aluminium windscreen shades

    or

- place blankets or towels – wet if possible – against inside of windows.
- Activate windscreen wipers to dislodge hot ash.
- Have fire extinguisher or water sprayer handy.
- Hunch down on seat or floor.
- Breathe through wetted towel or corner of blanket.
- Drink frequently.
- Spray water on occupants.
- While flames are over 1 m high it will be more dangerous outside than inside.
- Stay in car/shelter until you can see, by blackened ground, that the fire has moved on.
- **Exit only now.**
- Wait until smoke has cleared before driving off.
- Drive *away* from fire, even if this is not the direction of your destination.
- Drive away with lights on, through burnt areas only.
- Never drive or walk into an area that could still burn.

What can happen while you are in the car

- Petrol tank will only explode if the fuel in it is a precise 14% mixture ratio.
  - ➢ It won't explode in the short sheltering time needed in grass or mild forest fire.
- The petrol filler cap may be blown off by unvented tanks and petrol fumes may burn.
  - ➢ This is not dangerous.
- Diesel fuel has a lower flammability than petrol and won't explode.
- LPG cylinders won't explode. In extreme heat, pressure relief valves vent harmlessly.
  - ➢ LPG cylinders of cars burnt out in Black Saturday fires did not explode.
- Tyres may burn and burst or rupture with a loud, explosive noise.
- Windows may break and burning debris set fire to upholstery.
  - ➢ Cover windows with blanket or foil.
- Items of trim on the car may catch alight.
- Toxic gases may be released by overheated fittings and incapacitate you.
  - ➢ This can be avoided by car being in a wide enough, cleared area.
- In a grass fire or *mild* forest fire a car won't ignite before you can safely exit.

If forced out of the car by heat or fumes before the fire front passes

- Close the car completely to prevent internal ignitions.
- Cover yourself completely with pure wool blanket.
- Lie flat under the car or on a grass-free road surface or ditch, *not* on bitumen
  or
- keep the car between you and the flames as a radiant heat shield.

What can happen once the fire front has passed

- Grass and undergrowth could be blackened and therefore safe.
- Tree trunks around you may still be on fire.
  - ➢ Tree trunk flames burning disconnectedly are not dangerous.
  - ➢ Shelter from their heat beside car, protected by pure wool blanket.
- There may be thick smoke for hours.
  - ➢ Wear wet nose mask, and instil drops of artificial tears in your eyes.

A motel on a wide and clear highway could be a good refuge.
A rambling old guesthouse tucked into a bush setting may not.

Holiday accommodation as a refuge

- A downstairs room exiting onto a cleared area can provide safe shelter.
  - ➤ Do not shelter in an upstairs room.
  - ➤ Do not shelter in a room with only an internal exit door.
- Park your car in front of your door if space is provided.
  - ➤ Car can be a radiant heat shield if you need to exit the room.
- Pack your luggage.
  - ➤ Keep it with you, or in your closed car, covered with blanket.
- Put on protective clothing.
- Take with you to the shelter room:
  - ➤ Pure wool blanket, mobile phone and battery-operated radio.
  - ➤ Drinking water.
- When in shelter room, close windows and doors.
- Obtain resort manager's cooperation in safety procedures.
  - ➤ Have someone at windows and door with hose, water sprayers or wet mops. (See Chapter 21, What to do when bushfire threatens)

If holiday accommodation is not suitable as refuge

- Go to community refuge, solid public building, swimming pool or beach.
- Never try to escape by driving to another town while fire is in the area.

**Holiday-makers in a caravan park when a bushfire threatens
will be unlikely to have any hope of moving their caravan to a safer situation.**

Caravaners

- A free-standing brick or stone shower block can provide safe shelter.
- Put on protective clothing.
- Dismantle canvas annexe and put inside van.
- Close windows.
- Roll down caravan stone shields.
- Take down curtains and put them in cupboard.
- Drape wet blankets or towels on windows.
- Cover yourself with pure wool blanket and go to shower block.
- Do not try to escape by driving caravan out.
  - ➤ The chaos of mass caravan exodus can be lethal.

Campers

- Do not attempt to drive out unless you are certain of a safe, unhindered exit to a refuge.
- Put on protective clothing.
- Pack up tent and shelter with it in campsite shower block.
- Take refuge in a car only if it can be easily parked in lee of shower block or on beach.

Bushwalkers

- Don't walk in forests on days of high bushfire danger.
- Obtain local rangers' advice on whether it is safe to be in the area.
- Plan a safe route.
- Take protective clothing and pure wool blanket or aluminium foil tent.
- Take plenty of drinking water.
- Take a mobile phone.
    - ➤ Put the local fire authority and police phone numbers into phone address book.
- Take a reflector such as mirror or piece of tin and a whistle, for emergency signalling.
- While walking, note safe shelter areas. Good shelters are:
    - ➤ Caves.
    - ➤ Beneath overhanging ledges to the leeward of a fire, if bare of vegetation.
    - ➤ Creeks, pools or dams if banks bare of vegetation and bare ditches.
- Do not shelter in a water tank. (See Chapter 2, The killer factors)
- If it is a still day and you can see light smoke, walk away from it.
- If you see a fast-moving cloud of heavy smoke, find a nearby safe area and stay there.
- Phone your whereabouts to fire authority and police.
- If carrying flammable items, bury them and mark the spot.
- If embers fall, put on protective clothing.
- Cover yourself with pure wool blanket, foil tent or earth.
- Drink water or fruit juice often.
- When embers stop falling, phone authorities for advice on moving out.
- Move downhill and to the leeward of smoke.
- If you are with a group, keep together.
- Use tracks and roads where possible.
- Walk carefully. Don't run.
- Aim for burnt or bare ground.
- Keep away from dense vegetation.
    - ➤ Embers from any fire still burning could ignite this.

- Keep away from burnt trees, fallen fences and power lines.
  - ➤ Burnt trees can fall without warning.
  - ➤ Fallen fences may be electrified.
- Rest regularly.
- Try to signal your presence to any nearby authorities.
- When safe, inform fire authority and police.

**If you follow protective travelling rules
you are unlikely to be caught in a situation that makes your car unsafe as a refuge.**

20
Evacuate, defend or shelter?

Evacuating, defending and sheltering each have their own perils.
Either choice can lead to injury, death or survival.
Thorough knowledge and careful preparation are imperative for safety.

The ability to evacuate safely depends on

- Early enough warning of potential fire danger near your area or your planned route.
- Freedom from responsibilities and restraints that could detain you at home or work.
- Severity and distribution of fires burning throughout your greater region or state.
- Severity of weather conditions, particularly of wind speed.
- Severity of ember shower and speed of fire front in your region.
- Ability to leave well before a fire starts in your area or near your planned route.
- Sufficient advance packing and storage of precious possessions.
- Distance to refuge, whether community shelter or private house.
- Rehearsal of evacuation along planned route.
- Having protective clothing, water, nose covers and pure wool blankets.
- A reliable car, and thorough knowledge of when and how to shelter safely in it.

The ability to defend safely depends on

- Distance from highly flammable vegetation in forest or garden.
- Distance from neighbours' buildings.
- Thorough preparation of grounds by plant arrangement and clearance of hazards.
- Thorough preparation of house and outbuildings to minimise ember entry.
- Frequent practice of emergency plans.
- Enough physical, mental and emotional strength and determination.

- Sufficient and suitable fire extinguishing resources.
  - ➤ Including a sprinkler system if possible.
- Severity and spread of ember shower and speed of flame front.
- Wearing protective clothing.
- Thorough knowledge of how to shelter safely if this becomes necessary.

The ability to shelter safely depends on

- Thorough preparation of house and grounds, protective clothing and knowledge.
- A shelter location that gives protection from radiant heat, smoke and toxic fumes.
- In-house shelter easily exited from a door that leads to a non-hazardous outside area.
- Limiting the time in house or shelter to its exposure to flame front.
- Ability to check safely from inside shelter what stage the fire has reached.
- Exiting from an inside shelter only after the peak of flames has passed.
  - ➤ Ability to exit to safe area outside. This is vital – house may ignite before this.
- Any outside shelter being sited well away from flammable vegetation.
- Wearing protective clothing.
- Having a pure wool blanket.
- Having water to drink.

Stay/Go data

- Defending, evacuating and sheltering can each be traumatic.
- On any day, staying can be dangerous to those unaware of bushfire dangers.
- On extreme days, staying can be life-threatening unless you are thoroughly prepared.
- On most days, well-prepared homes can provide safe shelter for 'stayers'.
  - ➤ Stayers who have died have usually not known how to do so safely.
- On most days, well-prepared people can safely defend well-prepared homes.
- Even on extreme days, thoroughly prepared people have saved their homes.
  - ➤ A great many have been safely saved even on the most catastrophic days.
  - ➤ This is a hidden fact:
    - – Seldom publicised by the media, through misplaced ideas of newsworthiness.
    - – Seldom divulged by those achieving it, through misplaced feelings of guilt.
- At least two able-bodied, well-prepared adults are usually needed to safely defend.
- Research shows the house survival rate more than doubles when someone is present.
  - ➤ If they are fit and know what to do, the house survival rate can be more than 90%.
- Early-enough and careful evacuation may provide personal safety.
  - ➤ But leaves your house vulnerable. Increased losses are almost inevitable.

- Research shows that more than twice as many unattended houses are destroyed.
- Historically, most deaths occur while evacuating through embers, flames or smoke.
- The close second highest is when people are outside and not protectively clothed.
- The third highest is when people shelter inside too far from an exit.

Black Saturday, 7 February 2009 fatalities data

A group of eminent bushfire scientists[2] conducted research into contributing factors. They found that:
- Very few of those who died had a comprehensive fire plan.
  - ➢ 34% had intended to stay and defend their properties.
  - ➢ 26% had intended to wait and see before committing to stay or go.
  - ➢ 8% had intended to stay at their property but to seek shelter.
  - ➢ 15% provided no evidence of any intention.
- Of the fatalities who had decided to stay and defend:
  - ➢ 20% were found to be well prepared.
    - − The criteria for 'preparation' was 'appropriate activity' an hour before the fire.
  - ➢ 14% had made some preparations.
- Of the fatalities who had decided to evacuate:
  - ➢ Under 1% were well prepared; lacking even a 'cue' to go to a known destination.
  - ➢ 5% had a vague idea of a destination and cue to go.
- 30% of fatalities showed some evidence of fire-fighting defence. Of these:
  - ➢ 5% were carrying out active defence at the time of their deaths.
  - ➢ 25% were classified as carrying out some or questionable defence.
- For 70% of people who died no evidence was found of any kind of defence.
- 69% of Black Saturday fatalities occurred while people were sheltering inappropriately:
  - ➢ 34% of all fatalities, in the house generally.
    - − Almost all of these, 27%, were in the bathroom.
  - ➢ 8% outside in a shed, spa, bunker or outhouse.
- 22% of Black Saturday fatalities occurred outside the house.
  - ➢ 15.6% outside a house.
  - ➢ 3% on roadways.
  - ➢ 3% near cars.
  - ➢ 0.4% in open land reserves.
- 14% of people who died were fleeing in cars or on foot without suitable clothing.
  - ➢ Total deaths amounted to 1.24% of the 14 000 residents of the bushfire areas.
- No data was obtained on how many people successfully defended their homes.

---

2   John Handmer, Saffron O'Neil and Damien Killalea, *Review of fatalities in the February 7, 2009, bushfires, Final Report.* Prepared for the Victorian Bushfires Royal Commission April 2010 (Bushfire CRC Centre for Risk and Community, 13 April 2010.)

> **Bushfire dangers vary greatly.**
> **From most fires, home defence is practicable and evacuation may be an over-reaction.**
> **In a few fires, home defence could be perilous and early evacuation would be wise.**

Benefits and hazards of staying or going

Benefits of staying

- You will be able to protect property and precious possessions.
- Your home is more likely to survive.
- You will have access to water to prevent dehydration.
- Home conveniences.
- Children and the old are less likely to suffer heat exhaustion or dehydration at home.
- When a bushfire is near, danger from staying is usually less than from going.

Hazards of staying

- Stayers in houses with unmanaged surrounding vegetation can be endangered. (See Chapter 8, A protective garden)
- Stayers sheltering in houses not modified to resist ember attacks can be endangered. (See Chapter 9, A protective house design)
- Stayers engaged in outside defence without protective clothing have a high risk of death.
- Stayers who are too frail to carry out defence procedure can be endangered.
- Stayers who have little knowledge of how to stay safely can be:
  - ➤ Killed by radiant heat if they venture close to flames.
  - ➤ Killed by radiant heat if they are on a roof during a shower of embers.
  - ➤ Burnt by falling embers.
  - ➤ Endangered by unseen ignitions inside the house if not alert to entering embers.
  - ➤ Overcome by toxic gases from smouldering furnishings.
  - ➤ Trapped in an inner room or passageway, too far from a safe exit door.

> **Late evacuation, and defending or sheltering without thorough knowledge,**
> **can lead to injury or death.**
> **Especially if no protective clothing is worn.**

Voluntary evacuation

- By organising evacuation yourself, you can:
  - ➢ Choose a convenient safe time to go.
  - ➢ Arrange optimum time to prepare your vacated house.
  - ➢ Arrange to evacuate all the family.
  - ➢ Arrange to take children and frail family members to safety the night before.
  - ➢ Be freer to have fit family members home for defence.

Mandatory or mass evacuation

Precautionary mass evacuation – hazards

- Severe bushfire weather can be foretold, but not where bushfires will develop.
  - ➢ Entire rural regions could be emptied.
  - ➢ Official arrangements are seldom made for the relocation of populations.
  - ➢ Not everyone has family or friends to go to in a non-vulnerable town.
- Nobody can predict which towns would be non-vulnerable on any severe day.
  - ➢ Cities or very large towns are the only certainties.
- By removing potential defenders, those unable to leave are more endangered.
  - ➢ These would include hospital staff, local officials, carers at animal refuges.
- With few left to douse embers, house-to-house ignitions can destroy towns.
- Post-bushfire reconstruction costs are multiplied.
- Personal trauma from home losses is maximised when evacuations are maximised.

Emergency mass evacuation

- It is seldom possible to order such evacuation in time for it to be orderly and safe.
  - ➢ Too many at the same time on the same roads hazardous with smoke and fallen trees.
- Mass evacuation, by its very nature, leaves whole towns abandoned to destruction.
- Burning houses produce embers that ignite other houses.
  - ➢ In Canberra 2003, 30% of burnt homes were destroyed by house-to-house embers.
  - ➢ Most of those houses had been forcibly evacuated.

**Evacuees often say, 'It doesn't matter about the house'.
But it matters afterwards.**

Benefits of evacuation

To a near neighbour's safer house

- Not far to go.
- You can return home very soon after the fire to douse ignitions.

To a large town

- More likelihood of achieving safety from a bushfire.
- The less flammable the private gardens and nearby bush, the safer the town.
- Ignition is usually limited to outer houses of defended and vegetally managed towns.
  - ➢ The usual cause of destructions further in is undefended house-to-house ignition.
- Indoor, cool shelter is usually available in a public building or large store.
  - ➢ This is not satisfactory if the emergency continues overnight.
- A friend's house is most satisfactory if you may stay and bring pets.
  - ➢ Be aware that if your own house burns, you may need to stay indefinitely.

To a suitable community refuge

- You may have more shelter than at home.
  - ➢ This is not necessarily so.
- You may have the protection of firefighters.
  - ➢ This cannot be relied upon. All fire units may well be deployed elsewhere.

Hazards of evacuation

- *Official warnings* can be given too late to leave safely.
- *Personal decisions* to leave can be made too late to leave safely.
  - ➢ Radiant heat overcomes exposed pedestrians; cars crash in smoke. (See Chapter 19, Protective travelling)
- Families with no car of their own have extra difficulties. Possible options are:
  - ➢ Leaving by train the afternoon before predicted days of bushfire danger.
  - ➢ Having a city friend collect you the afternoon before the predicted day.
- People who can normally rely on others for transport, may not be able to do so that day.
  - ➢ If your usual 'lift' decides to stay, you will need to arrange another means of leaving.
  - ➢ If they do evacuate, they may not have room in their car for you and your possessions.
- There is seldom just 'a bushfire'; multiple fires can threaten from unknown locations.
- Your unattended home is more likely to be destroyed.

- You risk years in uncomfortable emergency accommodation.
    - ➢ The state's housing stock decreases and its homeless list increases.

To a near neighbour's house

- Even the short trip to a neighbour's can expose you to radiant heat and embers.
    - ➢ Especially if you are on foot.

To a large town

- Evacuees to large towns or refuges commonly underestimate travelling time.
- Evacuation route could be closed, blocked by fallen trees, stalled cars or fire units.
- You could crash because of smoke.
- Heat-caused vaporisation in the carburettor could stall older cars.
    - ➢ You could be trapped in a traffic jam of other evacuees.
- Children, the elderly, the frail and pets are can become ill in a hot car.
- Wind and fire direction may change without warning, showering embers on route.
    - ➢ In wild weather, even small spot fires will become fast-moving and dangerous.
    - ➢ Route can be cut off.
- Emergency pull-over places along roads are scarce.
- Fittings in the car can become unbearably hot and force you out.
    - ➢ Radiant heat from bush burning along the road can then kill you.

To a community refuge

- All the above points.
- Refuge may not be safer than your house.
- Most do not open for shelterers until fire danger has become apparent.
    - ➢ This stage is usually too dangerous to be travelling to it.
- Potential legal liability prevents authorities from guaranteeing your safety there.
- Protection by a fire unit is not guaranteed.
- There may not be facilities for care of children and the frail.
- There may not even be water on tap.
- Pets may not be allowed.
- There may not be safe parking for cars.
- Allowable time at a community refuge may be limited.
    - ➢ It could be available for no more than two to three hours.

- If refuge is an open space, smoke and embers may make being there unbearable.
  - ➤ You may be tempted to drive off from it into more dangerous conditions.
- Destination may not be any safer than home.
- Evacuees can be re-evacuated from destination.

Somewhere else may not be safer.
People with knowledge can survive in their own well-prepared houses.

Safe evacuation times

- A day of bushfire danger cannot always be anticipated.
  - ➤ Many bushfires happen on days for which no danger has been forecast.
  - ➤ An advance safe evacuation time may therefore not be available.
- Your home can suddenly become endangered at any time of day from fire started by:
  - ➤ Sparks from machinery being worked in grass or crops.
  - ➤ Children playing with matches in nearby bush or scrub.
  - ➤ Deliberate arsonists – this can happen very early in the morning.
  - ➤ Lightning strikes and flare-ups of old fires – this can happen at night.
- When bushfire weather *is* forecast, the only truly safe time to go is on the previous day.
- The 'leave before 10 a.m.' advice cannot guarantee safety.
  - ➤ Remote rural evacuees with a city destination may still be travelling after noon.
- It is not safe to wait for an official warning of when to leave.
  - ➤ It can be impossible for official warning to be given with time to leave safely.
  - ➤ Warning systems are subject to inaccuracies, failure and human error.
- It is not safe to plan exit time by radio, TV or internet postings on the bushfire situation.
  - ➤ Bulletins can become dangerously out of date very quickly.
  - ➤ It is best to combine official information with your own observations.
  - ➤ Electric power may be disconnected or disrupted by downed lines during a bushfire.
- It is vital to be aware of what is happening outside your own window.
  - ➤ A light, lazy smoke plume in the distance can give comfortable time to go.
  - ➤ A dense black cloud rapidly approaching warns of great danger in going.
- It is *usually* safe to go when home, route and destination are beyond ember-reach.
  - ➤ This will vary with wind force, vegetation type and density, and topography.
- Safe evacuation includes leaving your house as ember-safe as possible.

Evacuation to a bushfire shelter must be a preplanned bushfire response, not a 'last resort'.
A more effective, travel-free, 'shelter of last resort' is a pure wool blanket.

Safe evacuation procedure

- Allow time to tidy grounds and seal the house. (See Chapter 21, What to do when bushfire threatens, 'When bushfire weather is forecast')
  - ➢ Prepared homes have a good chance of being intact on evacuees' return.
- Store precious possessions in advance, out of the fire danger area.
- Leave the night before bushfires are expected, or at the first sign of light smoke.
  - ➢ Do not wait until embers fall.
- Know exactly where you are going and that you can get there safely.

Before leaving

- Put on protective clothing. (See Chapter 3, The survival factors)
- Put stock in a safe refuge paddock.
- If precious possessions not already stored, bury them. (See Chapter 14, Planning ahead)
- Save computer files to hard drive or memory stick.
  - ➢ Safer to bury them now than take them in a hot car.
- Put shutters over windows.
- Connect hoses. Fill containers with water and place them around house.
  - ➢ Someone else may use them to douse an ignition.
- Clear guttering of leaves if safe to do so. Stop downpipes. Fill gutters with water.
- Ask a neighbour to activate sprinklers (if any) when embers start to fall.
  - ➢ Be aware that in the emergency the neighbour may not be able to do this.
  - ➢ Do not do this yourself before leaving as water may be used up before fire arrives.
- Move flammable furniture away from windows and from other furniture.
- Cover flammable furniture with pure wool blankets or heavy rugs.
- Close internal doors.
  - ➢ Seal with non-flammable draught-stoppers or rolled-up, wetted towels.
- Close outside doors, but leave house unlocked.
  - ➢ Neighbours or firefighters may want to enter to douse small internal ignitions.
- Shut off gas and electricity at the mains.

Leaving

- Put survival kits and drinking water in car for you and pets.
- Put in pure wool blankets or foil tent for each evacuee, including pets.
- Put pets in car – dog on leash, cats/birds in cage, water and wool covers for them.
- Take drinking water, medication, mobile phone and battery-powered radio.
- Drive with car windows up, vents closed and headlights on.
- Carry out all procedures listed in Chapter 19, Protective travelling.
- Return as soon as possible after fire front has passed, to douse spot fires.
  - This can increase chances of house survival by 15–30%.
  - You must obey any police roadblock instructions.

Dangerous evacuation procedure

- Leaving:
  - When smoke envelops your property.
  - When embers are falling.
  - When you can see flames.
- Leaving dressed in light, unprotective clothing.
- Leaving with no drinking water.
- Not knowing where you are going.
- Leaving your house with windows or doors open.
- Leaving with pets chained or confined in pens.

Of those who died on Black Saturday, 14% fled by car or on foot during the threat. Of those who had planned to evacuate, less than 1% had well prepared plans. There was no evidence that anyone who followed safe evacuation practice died.

Safe defending procedure

- Put on protective clothing. (See Chapter 3, The survival factors)
- Carry out procedures in Chapter 21, What to do when bushfire threatens.

Safe sheltering procedure

- Go inside.
- Put on protective clothing.
- Keep mobile phone with you.
- Listen to battery-operated radio if possible.

- Close windows.
- Close internal and external doors.
- Shelter by an exit door, preferably one sheltered from wind-blown embers.
  - Do not shelter in an inner room.
  - Do not shelter in the bath.
- Drink water or fruit juice every 10 minutes.
- Keep watch through a small window or spy-hole to check the progress of the fire.
- Stay inside only while flames are fierce, usually no more than 15 minutes. (See Chapter 21, What to do when bushfire threatens, 'After the fire front has passed')

Hazardous sheltering procedure

- Sheltering in an inner room, passageway or bathroom.
  - Over a quarter of those who died on Black Saturday were sheltering in bathrooms.
- Sheltering in spas or water tanks.
  - When water reaches 42°C, a person loses consciousness and can drown.
- Sheltering in cellars.
  - Floor above can collapse onto you.
  - Toxic gases from burning materials can leak into them.
- Sheltering in sheds and non-standard bunkers.
  - Even if the structure does not burn, toxic gases may kill.
- Wearing only flimsy summer clothes.
- Not wearing a nose cover.
- Sheltering inside too long, such as for the whole duration of the bushfire.
- Exiting onto an area still burning fiercely.

**When in doubt, don't go:
shelter safely.**

Making the decision to evacuate, defend or shelter

- The decision must be pre-planned well before the bushfire season.
  - Very few of those who died on Black Saturday had a thorough fire plan.
- Your plan must take into account your bushfire authority's regulations.
  - Do the regulations allow you the right to defend your home?
  - Do they require you to obey an order to evacuate? If so, by whose order?
  - Check if this contravenes State law on your legal right to protect your property.

- Involve every member of your family in making the decision.
  - ➤ Children need to know your plans for them.
  - ➤ Children need to grow up with an awareness of safe bushfire activities.
- Together, discuss this chapter. (And see Chapter 5, The home as haven; Chapter 14, Planning ahead, 'Personal safety'; Chapter 19, Protective travelling; Chapter 21, What to do when bushfire threatens).
- Decide whether *all* the family is to evacuate, defend or shelter.

If your plan is to evacuate

- Will you all leave together, or children the night before and adults on the day?
- Set out every detail of the logistics of leaving for a safe place at a safe time. (See Chapter 14, Planning ahead, 'If you plan to evacuate')

If your plan is to stay

- Will everyone actively defend?
- Will some defend and others shelter by exit door, in a refuge room or bunker?
- Will some of the family be evacuated?
- Will the person taking them stay with them or return to defend?

Whatever you decide

- Ascertain whether your house insurance has bushfire damage exclusions.
- Obtain sufficient pure wool blankets and properly fitting protective clothing.
- Discuss your ideas with your *local* bushfire authority.
  - ➤ Will a warning device, such as a siren or app, alert you to a local bushfire?
  - ➤ Does the community have a phone-tree for emergency communication?
  - ➤ Is there a nearby community refuge readily available?
- Write down your plan.
  - ➤ Intending evacuees need an alternative 'Plan B', to stay safely. (See Chapter 21, What to do when bushfire threatens, 'If your plan is to shelter)
- Display your plan where all the family can easily see it.
- Talk about your plan often throughout the bushfire season.
- Practise your plan frequently throughout the year.

(See *The Complete Bushfire Safety Book*, The decision – evacuate or stay? Safety or suicide?)

**Whether evacuating, defending or sheltering,
any action taken without a thorough knowledge of how to do so safely,
can result in injury or death.**

21
What to do when bushfire threatens

To help your decisions

- The Bureau of Meteorology assesses the level of danger posed by weather conditions.
  - ➤ These levels are called Fire Danger Ratings.
- New Fire Danger Ratings were introduced following Victoria's February 2009 fires.
  - ➤ Be aware that they could be changed again.

Fire danger ratings

- **Moderate, High and Very High:** Mild to unpleasantly hot and windy.
  - ➤ If a fire starts, it can most likely be controlled and homes can provide safety.
- **Extreme and Severe:** Extremely hot, dry and windy conditions.
  - ➤ If a fire starts and takes hold, it will be uncontrollable, unpredictable and fast.
  - ➤ Spot fires will start, move quickly and come from many directions.
- **'Code Red' or 'Catastrophic':** The worst-known conditions for a fire.
  - ➤ Rare. More likely during drought.
  - ➤ Exceptionally hot day; unusually violent, gusty winds; extremely dry air.
  - ➤ Often a violent cool wind change is expected, which can dramatically increase danger.

All summer

- Be – and stay – prepared, well ahead of official warnings.
  - ➢ Water containers filled, and set around the house.
  - ➢ Throwing dippers, sprayers and mops available in an instant.
  - ➢ Protective clothing for a survival kit checked and handy.
  - ➢ Precious possessions stored, packed or otherwise made safe.

When bushfire weather is forecast

- Take small children, the aged and frail to your pre-arranged safe area.
  - ➢ This is the safest time for *any* evacuees to leave.
- Cancel unnecessary country trips.

However:

- If you have a country property, go there now to make it safe.
- Move stock into their refuge area. (See Chapter 18, Protecting domestic animals, stock and sanctuaries)
  - ➢ Do not leave this task until embers start falling.
- Clear under the house of flammables.
- Rake grounds clear of flammables.
- Bring in outdoor furniture, hanging baskets, mats, toys.
- Move plastic pots from flammable walls.
- Clear litter from forks of trees. Strip loose bark.
- Mow any long grass.
  - ➢ Bury rakings and grass clippings in mulch heap.
- Check for, and fix, loose tiles or roofing sheets.
- Prepare window covers. (See Chapter 9, A protective house design)
- Prepare covers for evaporative air conditioner intake and internal vents.
- Check survival kits.
- Connect nozzle-activated hoses to taps.
- Attach pump to reserve water and test that it works properly.
  - ➢ Don't rely on sophisticated appliances alone.
  - ➢ Pumps and fire hoses that worked the night before may not work on the day.

- Fill troughs, stirrup pumps, knapsacks, garden sprayers, buckets.
    - ➢ Containers that can easily direct water in any direction are most efficient.
    - ➢ Buckets are inefficient; they strain muscles and aim is often inaccurate.
- Put throwing dippers, mops or hessian bags in buckets, troughs, bath.
- Place these around buildings at windows, wall angles, subfloor, gaps, ceiling space.
- Set ladder, water-filled sprayers and torch at ceiling space inspection hole.
- Clear gutters.
- Block downpipes, fill gutters with water.
- Set ladder against roof on leeward side.
- If not already done, take precious possessions to a friend's safe house
  or
- put in refuge room or hired locker
  or
- bury in a garden dugout.
- Be aware that homes have been safely saved even on the most extreme days.

**It is not always possible to be given official advance warning of bushfires.
They can happen unexpectedly: from escaped burn-offs, lightning strikes, arson.
Look out the window. Smell the air. Notice the wind.
Be watchful and well-prepared *every* day of the season.**

Early on day of bushfire danger

Whether your plan is to *go*, *stay* or *shelter*, inform neighbours of your intention.

If your planned decision is to evacuate

- Recharge mobile phones.
- Back up computer to memory stick or portable external hard drive.
- Recharge laptop computers, iPods, iPads.
- Check that house is sealed.
- Close inside and outside doors of house.
    - ➢ To reduce fire flow from internal ignitions.
- Leave doors unlocked.
    - ➢ In case firefighters need to enter to extinguish fire.
- Wear, or have handy, protective clothing and wetted smoke mask.
- Have pure wool blankets in car.
- Have protective goggles ready around neck.
- **Go now.** (See Chapter 20, Evacuate, defend or shelter?, 'Safe evacuation procedure')

If your planned decision is to stay

- If any actions in 'When bushfire weather is forecast' have not been done, do them now.
- Check where family members intend to be during the day.
- If children's school has not been made bushfire-safe, keep them with you.
  - ➤ Not at home alone.
- Check through emergency action plans with each person.
- Bring pets close to the house. Put collars on dogs. Have leashes handy.
- Prepare cat cages.
- Move livestock to stock refuge. Check their water.
- Remove paddocked horses' metal shoes, rugs, fly-veils and halters.
- Clear straw from floor of concrete refuge stables. (See Chapter 18, Protecting domestic animals, stock, and sanctuaries)
- If precious possessions aren't already safe, cover with blankets or foil, or bury.
- Save computer files to hard drive or memory stick.
- Monitor battery radio, internet or rural brigade listening set for bushfire bulletins.
- Do not depend on internet or apps.
- It is vital to monitor your own environs.
  - ➤ Look out the window. Smell the air. Watch the wind.
  - ➤ Realise that electricity failure will cause computer or network to fail.
- Set ladder beside ceiling space inspection hole.
- Put water-filled containers and torch inside ceiling space.
- Put crawling planks across rafters.
- Leave ceiling space inspection hole open.
- Recharge mobile phones.
- Check radio batteries.
- Check that each window is clear of vegetation. If not, remove it.
- Cover skylights and evaporative air conditioning units with non-flammable covers.
- Check sheds so that flammable items are in covered, non-flammable containers.
- Check that gas cylinders vents face away from house.
- Fill bath and inside troughs to have ready water to douse embers that may enter house.
- Place water sprayers, mops in each room.
- Prepare drink flasks.

Smoke reduces visibility.
Eyes can be irritated, stinging can cause a feeling of confusion.
Allergies and asthma can be triggered.

Smoke is seen

- Report it to fire authority.
- Contact family and/or workers, advise of danger and check where each will be.

If your plan is to evacuate

- Leave no later than now. (See Chapter 20, Evacuate, defend or shelter?, 'Safe evacuation procedure')
- If conditions turn out to be too dangerous to leave as planned, shelter now. (See 'If you plan to shelter', below)
- Safe evacuation cannot be guaranteed at this stage.
  - ➤ The fire could escalate.
  - ➤ You could be trapped on the road by fallen trees.

If your plan is to stay

- Move stock safely to their refuge. (See Chapter 18, Protecting domestic animals, stock, and sanctuaries)
  - ➤ Do not endanger your life by doing this while embers are falling.
- If actions in 'Early on day of bushfire danger' above have not been done, do now.
- Put cars and other vehicles in a solid garage.
- Close car and garage completely
  or
- move vehicles to cleared area and if possible cover with heavy-duty foil.
- Seal house and sheds, close windows, doors.
- Cover windows with shutters, corrugated iron or heavy-duty foil. (See Chapter 9, A protective house design)
- Cover internal vents of evaporative air conditioner.
- Cover aviaries with foil or wet cloths. Bring bird cages inside.
- Bring pets inside. If you have a refuge room, put them there.
  - ➤ Dogs with collars on and leashes handy, cats in covered cages.
  - ➤ Cover pet horse's face with a cloth. (See Chapter 18, Protecting domestic animals, stock and sanctuaries)
- Take in outdoor furniture, doormats, hanging baskets, plastic pot plants.
- If windows unshuttered:
  - ➤ If curtains are pure wool, close them.
  - ➤ If not, take them down and put into cupboard.
  - ➤ Cover windows with pure wool blankets, heavy-quality quilts, foil or wet towels.
- Move flammable furniture away from windows.
- Cover flammable furnishings with pure wool blankets, heavy quilts.

- Put small flammables, cushions, papers into cupboards.
  - ➤ To reduce the opportunities for rapid ember ignition.
- Fill bath and troughs with water for dousing embers.
- Put water containers in each room, with sprayers, dippers, mops.
- Clear gateways, driveways, doorways and around windows.
- Watch vigilantly for falling embers.

The shower of embers can arrive half an hour before the fire front. And can keep falling for four hours after the main fire has passed.

The shower of embers

Ember data

- Embers can be blown from either the bushfire or from already burning houses.
- Embers can be blown from:
  - ➤ Eucalypts –4 km.
  - ➤ Pine trees – 2.5 km.
  - ➤ Grass –100 m.
- Firebrands can be blown from:
  - ➤ Candle or stringy-bark – 8–35 km
- Both firebrands and embers fall:
  - ➤ Thickly within 100 m of a flame front.
  - ➤ Thinly further than 3 km from a fire front.
- They can start fresh fires in any flammable substance.
- They can enter houses in small numbers, flare slowly and be easily doused
  or
- mass though a broken window or lifted roof and destroy a house quickly and violently.
- They can fall on people and cause life-threatening burns.

If your plan is to evacuate

- It is too late to evacuate now. Activate safe sheltering plan (see below).
  - ➤ Historically, most people who die in a bushfire are killed at this stage.
- Wear protective clothing and wetted smoke mask.
- Have protective goggles ready around neck.
- Check that house is sealed. (See 'Smoke is seen', above)

- Turn off air conditioners.
- Close internal doors.
- Wet towels, bags, roll them up and place at door gaps and window ledges.
- Have enough wet towels, gel neckties, to help cool family by draping round necks.
- If you have a bushfire sprinkler system, activate it now.
  - ➤ It is a waste of water and your time to do this before embers fall.
- Activate sprinklers on stables and fowl sheds. (See Chapter 18, Protecting domestic animals, stock, and sanctuaries)
- If you have a refuge room, settle children/frail/pets here with blankets and water.
- Shut off gas and electricity at the mains.
- Plug keyholes with playdough, blue-tack, plasticine or soap.

If your plan is to defend

- It is too late now to perform outdoor actions.
- Complete indoor preparations in 'If your plan is to say', above.
- Turn off air conditioners.
- Check that external doors and windows are closed.
- Put on full protective clothing.
- **Go outside.**
- Stay close to your house.
- Wet lawns and fireward sides of house.
- Watch particularly for sparks/embers in ceiling space, subfloor, on window ledges, roof.
- Douse embers as they land.
- You need deal *only* with embers on and by the house and in the nearby garden.
- Do not go beyond your own garden to fight spot fires.
- Do not approach fire in the bush or coming uphill.
  - ➤ The radiant heat from 1.5 m flames causes unbearable pain within a minute.
  - ➤ Radiant heat from a flame front 40 m away can kill.
- If dousing flame, aim water *at the burning substance* not at the flame itself.
- Do not stamp out flames.
  - ➤ People have died from ignited trousers.
- If your house has no roof sprinklers:
  - ➤ Have one fit, protectively clothed person on ladder to douse roof.
  - ➤ Concentrate water on the hips and hollows of roof and on gutters.
- Roof defender must come down before a fire front arrives.
  - ➤ **This is vital.**
- Drink frequently. Intersperse water with fruit juice.
  - ➤ Too much water can upset the electrolyte balance of the blood.
- Insert artificial tears or eye gel into eyes frequently.

If your plan is to shelter

- Put on protective clothing.
- Put vehicles in a solid, closed garage or cleared area.
- **Go inside.**
- Close windows, internal and external doors.
- Turn off air conditioners.
- Seal the house and follow preparatory points as above.
- Drink water every 10 minutes, or eat juicy fruit.
- If able, douse any entering sparks and embers with water sprayer or wet mop. (See below, 'The fire front arrives' – 'While inside')
  - ➤ Watch for embers in ceiling space, windows, gaps under doors.
  - ➤ If thorough house preparation has been done, these will be unlikely, or few.
- Shelter by an exit door, preferably one sheltered from the wind.
  - ➤ Not in the hallway. Not in the bath. You must be able to exit quickly and safely.
  - ➤ In protective clothing, with pure wool blanket. (See below)
- Watch progress of the fire through a small window or door peephole.
- Stay inside only while flames are fierce, usually no more than15 minutes.
- When you see that flames have died down, it is safe to go outside.
  - ➤ Tree trunks burning with disconnected flames are not a danger.
- It is vital for passive shelterers to exit now.
  - ➤ Embers could have ignited unseen in ceiling space, subfloor or wall cavities.

**A fire front can be a wall of flame higher than trees, or scampering through short grass.
It depends on the density and combustibility of vegetation.
Respect all flames. High or low, fast or slow, they can kill and maim.**

The fire front arrives

If the house has ignited ahead of the fire front

- Do not run or drive away. Flames from burning fine fuel will soon die down.
  - ➤ Fire flares and diminishes as that fuel is consumed.
- Life-threatening radiant heat is unlikely when flammable vegetation has been reduced.
- Shield yourself beneath pure wool blanket or foil tent.
  - ➤ Wet only the portion of blanket covering your nose, to facilitate breathing.
  - ➤ A completely wetted blanket has neither hazard nor benefit.

- Shelter behind a wall or large fire-resistant tree
  or
- in or beside the car if no vegetation is nearby and windows are closed
  or
- crouch on a bare or already burnt area.

If the house has not ignited

- **Go inside.**
  - ➤ Go in by a leeward entrance so blowing embers will not follow you in.
- Take hose, sprayers and ladder inside with you.
- Close the door behind you.
- Stay in protective clothing, but loosen it around neck and sleeves.
- If smoke has penetrated house, wear wetted nose cover.

The Pattern of Protection is Outside, Inside, Outside.

While inside

Active sheltering

- Watch for invading embers.
- Guard ceiling space, windows and doors with prepared water facilities.
- Check the ceiling space frequently for spark entry and smouldering material.
- Quickly spray or hit with wet mop any sparks, embers or smouldering.
- If an ignition cannot be extinguished, close the door of that room.
- Maintain access to an exit door.
- Never go outside during a flame front to douse an ignition.

Passive sheltering

(See Chapter 20, Evacuate, defend or shelter?, 'Safe sheltering procedure')
- Wear protective clothing.
- Keep pure wool blankets and drinking water next to you.
- Stay by an exit door, preferably one that is shielded outside.
- Do not shelter in an inner room, passageway
- Do not shelter in the bath.
  - ➤ Unnoticed embers in ceiling space, subfloor or wall cavities can take hold.
  - ➤ Suddenly flaming walls or a roof collapse can trap you.
  - ➤ A bath filled with water cannot save you.
    - – Its purpose is only for dousing embers and flames.

All shelterers

- Cool off when possible.
- Keep drinking water or fruit juice.
- Watch the condition of the fire through a small window or door peephole.
- Stay inside *only* until the peak of flames (the fire front) has passed the house.
    - ➤ For grass fires, this takes a minute or so.
    - ➤ For even fierce forest fires, this takes up to 15 minutes.
    - ➤ When surface flames die down, it's safe to go out again. (See below)

Never assume that because the fire front has passed you are safe from burning embers. They can fall, enter and ignite for a further three to four hours.

After the fire front has passed

- Realise that blackened ground and burnt vegetation is safe.
    - ➤ Burning tree trunks generally do not emit enough radiant heat to kill.
- Re-adjust loosened protective clothing. Wear nose cover.
- **Go outside**.
- Exit must be from a sheltered door or window.
- Exit with great care.
    - ➤ Wet clothes and nose cover, take drinking water.
    - ➤ Shelter beneath pure wool blanket, crouch, lower eyelids.
- Open door only a few centimetres at first, to check conditions.
    - ➤ If door opens onto a fiercely burning structure, exit could be perilous.
    - ➤ In this case, if house is safe, re-enter, shut hazardous door, use alternative exit.
    - ➤ If this is not safe to do, shield with blanket, turn sprayer on yourself and exit quickly. (See Chapter 17, Safe burn-offs, 'If trapped by flames')
- Close exit door or window behind you.
- Go to bare or blackened ground or the shelter of a large, fire-resistant tree.
- Keep checking the radiation level with some exposed skin.
- Look for and douse smouldering and ignitions.
    - ➤ Under house, on roof, in gutters, on window ledges, verandah.
    - ➤ Check where timber beams cross, such as on verandahs or pergolas.
    - ➤ Feel for hot spots on walls.
    - ➤ Wet around hot spots.
    - ➤ With water ready, break wall open quickly at the hottest spot, with axe, bar or pick.
    - ➤ Douse any fire quickly.

- When sure house is safe from external ignitions, check inside,
  - Have hose or water sprayer with you at all times.
  - Look for and douse any smouldering or ignition in ceiling space.
  - Check furnishings for any smouldering.
  - Feel for hot spots on skirting boards and walls; if any, proceed as for outside walls.
  - In ceiling space, around windows, on cushions, carpet, bedclothes.
- When sure house is safe from internal ignitions, return outside.
- Repeat internal check, frequently, over the next few hours.
  - Small ignitions often flare long after flame front has passed, and destroy a house.
- Check garage and outbuildings, car, tractors and machinery.
- Look for and douse smouldering vegetation.
- Attend to stock.
  - Spray water on live fowls and birds.
  - Do not rush to shoot injured or burnt animals. Their injuries may be treatable.
- Check fences for smouldering.
- Go over every centimetre of property, repeatedly.
- Check inside, repeatedly.
- If you must leave by car, do so only when smoke has cleared.
  - Check, if possible, with local fire authority if it is safe to do so.
- Inspect inside and out, day and night, until after all fires in your district are out.

**Even more important than defendable houses
is the *defendable ability* of householders.**

22
First aid for bushfire injuries

First aid is what you do at once before medical help is obtained.
It can make the difference between life and death.
Lives can be saved, and the effects of injuries minimised, with simple treatments.

The most common injuries sustained during a bushfire are

- Burns.
- Heat stroke.
- Heat exhaustion and heat cramps.
- Asphyxiation from breathing in smoke, superheated air or toxic fumes.
- Dehydration.
- Eye irritation by smoke or cinders.
- Sore throats from the effects of smoke and heat.
- Shock.

Bushfire first aid kit

- A packet of 5 cm gauze squares
  or
- some ironed cotton squares or white handkerchiefs in a clean plastic bag.
- A 5 cm gauze bandage.
- A 10 cm crepe bandage.
- Adhesive strapping.
- Scissors.
- Antiseptic such as Savlon wipes and spray, tea tree oil or aloe vera.

- Savlon cream or acriflavine.
  - ➤ For minor wounds and grazes.
- Burn creams such as Butesin Picrate.
- Burnaid gel-impregnated burn dressings.
  - ➤ Available in one-use sachets.
- Burnshield or Safety-Med gel-saturated blankets.
  - ➤ Can be wrapped around a person whose clothes are on fire.
  - ➤ Can be used as heat shields and to smother flames.
- Eye pads.
- Artificial tears.
- Recuperative drinks such as Staminade or Lucozade.
- Blanket for keeping shocked patient warm.
- Gel necktie cooler and/or vest for keeping heat stressed patient cool.
- *Bach Flowers* Rescue Remedy.
  - ➤ Helps to counteract shock, fear and emotional trauma.

Emergency treatment for all types of injury

- If the person is cold, cover with a blanket.
- If unconscious, lie them on one side with the head slightly down towards the chest.
- Do not try to resuscitate a collapsed person by getting them up and walking them.
- Give Rescue Remedy.
- When in doubt, seek medical help.

Burns affect not only the skin.
Skin is a respiratory organ that cannot function when burnt.
Skin is the wrapper that holds fluids inside the body – when burnt, the skin leaks fluid.
The main causes of death from burns are shock and infection.

Burns

Affect

- Lungs, blood circulation and kidneys can be involved.
- Fluid loss from 'weeping' burns can be great.
- Resultant imbalance of the body's minerals and salts can cause mental derangement.
- Burns to the surface of the skin can hurt more than deep burns.
- The most painful burns are not always the most serious.
- Deep burns are more likely than surface ones to become infected.

- Large surface burns are more life-threatening than a small deep burn.
- Even small burns to the hands, feet, genital area or face usually need hospitalisation.
- Any burn over 20% of the body endangers life.

Treatment

For any burn

- Never, never pull the clothes off a burnt person.
  - ➤ Pulling off stuck clothing pulls delicate tissue away with it.
- If it is necessary to remove clothing, and any is stuck to a burn, cut around it.
- Give Rescue Remedy.
- Wrap in a Burnshield or Safety-Med gel-saturated blanket.
- Cover the burnt person with a blanket or coat.
  - ➤ A burnt person's body can react by becoming dangerously cold (hypothermia).
  - ➤ This can be a first sign of clinical shock.
- Remove rings, bracelets or anything that could constrict the affected part.
- Give pain relief.
- Watch for signs of shock.

Surface burns

- Do not pull clothing off burn – cut around and leave it.
- Do not break blisters.
- Best initial first aid is to immediately apply ice.
- Next best is to run clean cold water over the burn for 10 minutes
  or
- apply a wrung-out wet cloth to burnt area.
- Apply Savlon spray, tea tree oil, aloe vera or Butesin Picrate.

Large or deep burns

- Apply Burnaid gel-impregnated dressings.
  - ➤ This cools the burn, relieves pain and helps prevent infection.
- Wrap the person in a Burnshield or Safety-Med gel-saturated blanket if available
  - ➤ Will prevent clothes sticking to burnt skin, ease pain and prevent infection.
  Or
- cover with clingwrap placed lengthways over the area
  - ➤ Do not wrap it tightly around the limb.
  Or
- cover burns with clean, dry, white dressing.
  - ➤ An unused, ironed white handkerchief will do, with its inner sides on the burn.

Heat stress on your body can cause failure of vital organs, collapse and death.
When this happens suddenly, it is called heat stroke.
The heat radiated from some fire front flames can kill this way within seconds.

Heat stroke

Symptoms

- Symptoms are dramatic and come on suddenly.
- Sweating stops and skin is hot and dry.
- Pulse is rapid and shallow.
- Breathing sounds like sighing.
- Vomiting.
- Aggression.
- Mental disturbance.
- Resisting assistance, denial that anything is wrong.
- Staggering, lack of limb co-ordination.
- Convulsions.
- Collapse and loss of consciousness.
    - This is a life-threatening situation.

Treatment

- Give Rescue Remedy.
- Immerse hands and arms in cold water of 10°C for 20 minutes.
    - This reduces core body temperature.
- Remove clothes.
- Fan the body.
- Wrap in wet sheets or towels
    or
- sponge all over with tepid water and let the water evaporate on the skin.
    - Do not immerse in a bath – evaporation is needed.
- If unconscious, turn the person onto one side, with the head slightly down.
- If the person becomes cold suddenly or fingers or lips are blue, remove cold packs.
- Cover with a blanket and obtain urgent medical help if safe to do so.
- Watch for signs of shock.

Heat exhaustion

Symptoms

- Looks pale and exhausted.
- Sweats profusely.
- Feels light-headed, giddy or faint.
- Feels stifled.
- Headache.
- Nausea
- Cramps.

Treatment

- Lie the person in a cool, airy place.
- Loosen and remove clothing.
- Give Rescue Remedy.
- Put a cool, wet pad on the forehead.
- Wet the hair.
- Sponge all over with cool water – allow the water to dry on the body by evaporation.
- Give glucose drinks, Staminade or a weak saline solution to sip.
- If the person is unable to drink, give ice to suck
  or
- drip fluid into the mouth from a dropper or by squeezing a wet cloth.
- If faint, elevate the lower part of the body.

Heat cramps can happen when the body loses salts and minerals through sweating. It is a common effect of dehydration.

Heat cramps

Symptoms

- Painful muscle spasms.

Treatment

- Gently stretch the affected muscle.
- Apply a heat pack.
- Massage muscle with eucalyptus, tea tree, rosemary, lavender oil or arnica
  or
- apply a compress of cider vinegar or peppermint leaves.
- Give 'sports' drinks, or water with a half a teaspoon of salt added per litre.

> The inhalation of superheated air can cause the inside of the throat to swell.
> The windpipe can be compressed very quickly.
> If this happens, the person can choke and can die.

Inhalation of smoke, superheated air and toxic fumes

Smoke inhalation

Symptoms

- Noisy breathing.
- Spasmodic coughing.
- Difficulty breathing, a feeling of choking.
- Disorientation.
- Death.

Treatment

- Sit the person up in the fresh air.
- Loosen clothing around the neck and chest.
- Apply mouth-to-mouth resuscitation or CPR if necessary.
- Seek medical help.

Superheated air

Symptoms

- The inside of the throat can swell.
- Wheezing, difficulty breathing.
- Redness of face.
- Choking.
  - ➢ This is a life-threatening situation.

Treatment

- Apply ice packs to the neck.
- If swelling allows, gargle gently with a weak saline solution.
- Obtain urgent medical help.

Toxic fumes

- The most common toxic gas inhaled during bushfire is hydrogen cyanide.

Symptoms

- Gasping very suddenly for air.
- Rapid breath.
- Fast heart rate changing to slow heart rate.
- Vomiting.
- Headache.
- Weakness.
- Confusion.
- Convulsions.
- Loss of consciousness.
- Respiratory failure leading to death.
    - ➤ This can happen very quickly.

Treatment

- Take the person outside into fresh air.
    - ➤ Cyanide gas disperses quickly in the open.
- Flush eyes with large amounts of tepid water or saline solution.
- Apply mouth-to-mouth resuscitation or CPR.
- Obtain urgent medical help.

Dangerous dehydration occurs when you excrete more fluid than you drink. During a bushfire, sweating can excrete 2 L of fluid an hour. Symptoms can start when 2% of your body's water volume has been lost.

Dehydration

Symptoms – progressive

- Sluggish movements.
- Irritability, impatience.
- Muddle-headedness, sleepiness.
- Hot, flushed dry skin.
- Nausea.
- Cramps.

- Inability to sweat.
  - ➤ Kidneys become severely stressed.
- Inability to pass urine; any excreted is scant and dark.
- Unconsciousness, becomes comatose.
- Death.

Treatment

- Give the person small drinks, often.
  - ➤ Do not add salt to the drink without professional advice.
- Cool the person as for heat stress.
- If the person has not passed urine for 12 hours, seek medical help.
- Watch for symptoms of shock.

Hot air can dry the eyes severely and cause ulcers that lead to blindness. Smoke can cause simple eye irritation or deposit sight-threatening cinders and grit.

Eye injuries

Symptoms

- Redness and watering of eye.
- Closing the eyelid.
- Blurred vision.
- Pain.
- Disorientation.

Treatment

- Do not rub eyes.
- Handle eyes only with very clean hands and materials.
  - ➤ Eyes are easily infected.

Irritated eyes

- Instil artificial tears or gel
  or
- rinse with boiled, tepid water.

Cinders or grit in the eye

- If object is on the white of the eye and not embedded, you may try to remove it.
  - ➤ By rinsing with a cool boiled water or a weak saline solution
  - or
  - ➤ by lifting it with the corner of a clean white handkerchief.
- Do not persist in trying to remove grit.
- Instil artificial tears or gel.
- Put a clean pad over the eye and secure it in place with a thin strip of adhesive.
- Do not put ointment in the eye.
  - ➤ Dust will cling to it, boosting the chance of infection.
- Obtain medical help as soon as possible.

Clinical shock is not the shock of fright.
Though shock is the body's way of trying to conserve life, it can cause death.

Shock

- Any injured person can go quickly into shock.
- External body functions start to shut down.
- If not treated quickly, this spreads to vital organs.

There are three stages of shock

1 The pulse is fast, blood pressure falls and extremities are cold.
2 The person has chest pain, becomes confused.
  - ➤ This stage of shock can be reversed.
3 The vital organs (kidneys, liver and heart) shut down.
  - ➤ This stage is irreversible, and the person dies.

Symptoms

- Extremities become cold.
- Lips and tips of fingers become blue.
  - ➤ Watch for onset of shock by feeling hands and feet.
- Pulse is rapid and weak.
- Breathing rapid and shallow.
- Blood pressure falls.
- Skin is cold and clammy.

- Mental confusion.

Until the above stage, treatment can save the person.

> It then becomes irreversible.

- Chest pain indicates heart is failing.
- The person dies.

Prevention and treatment

- Keep the person warm.
  > Especially the trunk area.
- Give Rescue Remedy.
- Massage hands, arms and feet gently towards the trunk of the body.
- Raise the lower part of the body 10–12 cm so that the feet are higher than the head.
  > Do not just lift the person's feet.
  > The aim is to encourage blood flow to vital organs such as the heart.
- Obtain urgent medical help as soon as possible.

Care and transport of a badly injured person

- Keep the person warm.
- Do not try to increase the blood circulation of a collapsed person by exercise.
  > This takes blood to muscles and skin – away from vital internal organs.
- Do not allow badly affected persons to walk.
- Carry a badly injured person gently, with six people if necessary.
  > Two at the shoulders, two at the hips and two at the legs and feet.
  > With arms linked under the patient by gripping each others' forearms.
- Drive as gently as possible – jolting increases pain and the chance of shock.
- Do not give any food to eat.
  > An operation under anaesthetic may be necessary.
- Restrict drinking to sips of water.

**If medical treatment is needed for anyone during a bushfire,
check first that the road is clear and safe before trying to drive to hospital.**

Bibliography

2009 Victorian Bushfires Royal Commission Final Report. Vol. I, *The Fires and Fire-related Deaths*.

2009 Victorian Bushfires Royal Commission Final Report. Vol. II, Parts 1 & 2, *Fire Preparation Response and Recovery*.

2009 Victorian Bushfires Royal Commission Final Report. Vol. IV, *Statements of Lay Witnesses*.

2009 Victorian Bushfires Royal Commission Final Report. *Summary*.

2009 Victorian Bushfires Royal Commission Interim Report. Auditor General Victoria.

2009 Victorian Bushfires Royal Commission (Melbourne). Submission from Robert Sproule, Drouin West, *Behaviour of Evaporative Air Conditioner*. SUBM.002.008.0152. Transcript, 22 April 2009.

2009 Victorian Bushfires Royal Commission (Melbourne). Transcript, 25 May 2009.

2009 Victorian Bushfires Royal Commission (Melbourne). Transcript, 29 May 2009.

2009 Victorian Bushfires Royal Commission (Melbourne). Transcript, 22 February 2010. Land and Fuel Management Expert Forum.

2009 Victorian Bushfires Royal Commission (Melbourne). Transcript 23 February 2010. Land and Fuel Management Expert Forum.

2009 Victorian Bushfires Royal Commission (Melbourne). Inquiry into the fire-related deaths – Kilmore East, Detective Superintendent Hollowood, Victoria Police. Transcript, 1 March 2010.

2009 Victorian Bushfires Royal Commission (Melbourne). Inquiry into the fire-related deaths – Kilmore East, Detective Superintendent Hollowood, Victoria Police. Transcript, 2 March 2010.

2009 Victorian Bushfires Royal Commission (Melbourne). Inquiry into the fire-related deaths – Kilmore East, Detective Superintendent Hollowood, Victoria Police. Transcript, 3 March 2010.

2009 Victorian Bushfires Royal Commission (Melbourne). Inquiry into the fire-related deaths – Kilmore East, Detective Superintendent Hollowood, Victoria Police. Transcript, 4 March 2010.

2009 Victorian Bushfires Royal Commission (Melbourne). Transcript, Hearing Block Five, 1 February–4 March 2010.

2009 Victorian Bushfires Royal Commission (Melbourne). Transcript, 27 April 2010.

2009 Victorian Bushfires Royal Commission (Melbourne). Transcript, 6 May 2010.

2009 Victorian Bushfires Royal Commission (Melbourne). Transcript, 7 May 2010.

2009 Victorian Bushfires Royal Commission (Melbourne). Transcript, 10 May 2010.

ABC1 television, 'Catalyst: In the Line of Fire'. Tozer family's home, Steele's Creek.

ABC Radio 774 'AM'. Report by Zoie Jones, 2 March 2009 quoting Robert Caulfield, Director, Australian Institute of Architects.

Age, 11 March 2009.

Animal Aid. *Plan, Prepare and Protect your Pets*. www.animalaid.org.au.

Australasian Fire and Emergency Service Authorities Council (2010) *Bushfires and Community Safety.* Position, Version 4.1. 8 September 2010.

Boura J (1999) Community Fireguard: creating partnerships with the community to minimise the impact of bushfire. *Australian Journal of Emergency Management* **13 (3)**, 59–64. Based on a paper originally presented at *inFIRE: Fire Information for the 21st Century.* International Network for Fire Information and Reference Exchange Conference, 4–8 May 1998, Melbourne.

Centre for International Economics (2011) 'Proposal to amend the Building Code of Australia to include requirements for private bushfire shelters'. Final regulation impact statement. January.

Centre for Risk and Community Safety (2006) *The Stay and Defend Your Property or Go Early Policy.* Fire Note, Issue 7, October. RMIT University, Melbourne.

Centre for Risk and Community Safety (2006) *A Legal Look at Stay and Defend or Go Early.* Fire Update, Issue 15. RMIT University, Melbourne.

Centre for Risk and Community Safety (2009) *Community Vulnerability Tested in 2003 Bushfires.* Fire Note, Issue 27, March. RMIT University, Melbourne.

Cheney P and Packham D (2009) *Don't Mention the FU.. word!* 7 October.

Cheney P (2010) Former Senior Principal Research Scientist, Bushfire Behaviour and Management Group, CSIRO. Personal communication, email 22 July.

Cheney P (2010) Former Senior Principal Research Scientist, Bushfire Behaviour and Management Group, CSIRO. Personal communication, email 25 July.

Cheney P (2010) Former Senior Principal Research Scientist, Bushfire Behaviour and Management Group, CSIRO. Personal communication, email 29 July.

Cheney P (2010) Former Senior Principal Research Scientist, Bushfire Behaviour and Management Group, CSIRO. Personal communication, email 22 November.

Cheney P (2010) Former Senior Principal Research Scientist, Bushfire Behaviour and Management Group, CSIRO. Personal communication, email 10 August.

Country Fire Authority Victoria (2003) Municipal fire prevention planning guidelines. First published May 1997.

Country Fire Authority Victoria (2009) Neighbourhood Safer Places: places of last resort during a bushfire. Interim assessment guidelines. Version 3.1, October.

Country Fire Authority Victoria (2010) Post-fire qualitative research. Final report on the analysis of Community Fireguard Group members' experience of the 2009 bushfires. April.

CSIRO Submission 09/355 (2009) *Bushfires in Australia.* Prepared for the 2009 Senate Inquiry into Bushfires in Australia. July.

Dart J (2009) 70 per cent prepared and 30 per cent luck: how David survived the inferno. *Sydney Morning Herald,* 16 February.

De Laine D, Pedler T, Probert J, Goodman H and Rowe C (2008) Fiery women: consulting, designing, delivering and evaluating pilot women's bushfire safety skills workshop. Conference presentation, Australasian Fire and Emergency Services Authorities.

Department of Sustainability and Environment. Wildfire Management Overlay. DSE, Melbourne.

Dowling J (2009) Log home stands as new building regulations come into effect today.

Dunlop C, Monson R and Handmer J (2006) *Shifting Risks and Responsibilities: The Balancing Exercise.* Outcomes of a workshop on the legal issues of 'stay or go' and community warnings in relation to community safety programs. Fire Note, Issue 6. Bushfire CRC, RMIT University, Melbourne.

Ellis P (2002) CSIRO Forestry and Forest Products. *The Adequacy of the Australian Standards AS3959-1999: Construction of Buildings in Bushfire-prone Areas.* Statement to Select Committee of the NSW Parliament on Bushfires. June.

Emergency Management Australia (1998) *Public Cyclone Shelter Study Greater Darwin Region.* Northern Territory, Australia.

Fire Protection Association Australia (2000) External water spray systems to aid building protection from wildfire. July. Sponsored by the Australian program for the UN International Decade for Natural Disaster Reduction 1990–2000.

Gill AM and Moore PHR (1996) *Ignitibility of Leaves of Australian Plants.* Centre for Plant Biodiversity Research, CSIRO Plant Industry, Canberra. Available online at: http://www.aff.org. au/AFF2_Gill&Moore_Final_ignitibility_of_leaves.htm

Gould IS, McCaw WL, Cheney NP and Matthews S (2007) *Fuel Assessment and Fire Behaviour Prediction in Dry Eucalypt Forest: A Field Guide.* Bushfire CRC interim edition.

Gould IS, McCaw WL, Cheney NP, Ellis PF, Knight IK and Sullivan AL (2007) *Project Vesta. Fire in Dry Eucalypt Forests: Fuel Structure, Fuel Dynamics and Fire Behaviour.* CSIRO Publishing, Melbourne.

Handmer J and Haynes K (2008) *Community Bushfire Safety.* CSIRO Publishing, Melbourne.

Handmer J and Tibbit A (2005) Is staying at home the safest option during bushfires? Historical evidence for an Australian approach. *Environmental Hazards* **6**, 81–91.

Handmer J, O'Neil S and Killalea D (2010) Review of fatalities in the February 7 2009 bushfires. Final Report. Bushfire CRC for Risk and Community Safety, RMIT, Melbourne. Prepared for the 2009 Victorian Bushfires Royal Commission, EXP.029.003.0001.

Haynes K (2009) 100 Years of Stay or Go. *Fire Australia* **Winter**, 30–32.

Haynes K and Tibbits A (2007) Evacuate late at your peril: an assessment of Australian bushfire fatalities. In *Proceedings of TASSIE FIRE Conference.* 18–20 July, Hobart. Centre for Risk and Community Safety, RMIT University, Melbourne and Risk Frontiers, Macquarie University, Sydney.

Haynes K, Tibbits A, Coates L, Ganewatta G, Handmer J and McAneney J (2008) 100 years of Australian civilian bushfire fatalities: exploring the trends in relation to the 'stay or go' policy. Report. Centre for Risk and Community Safety, RMIT University, Melbourne and Risk Frontiers, Macquarie University, Sydney.

Krusel N and Petris SN (1999) *A Study of Civilian Deaths in the 1983 Ash Wednesday Bushfires Victoria, Australia.* CFA Occasional Paper No. 1. Originally published as Staying alive: lessons learnt from a study of civilian deaths in the 1983 Ash Wednesday bushfires. *Fire Management Quarterly* **2** (16 December 1992), a supplement to *The Fireman.* Subsequently published June 1993in IAWF *Hotsheet* **2** (1), 3–19. Later presented at the 12th International Conference of Fire & Forest Meteorology. Georgia, October 1993.

Lands Alliance (2010) *Fuel Reduction Burning in Southern Australia's Forests: A Review of its Effectiveness as a Bushfire Management Tool.* Lands Alliance, Melbourne.

Lazarus G and Elley J (1984) *A Study of the Effect of Household Occupancy During the Ash Wednesday Bushfire in Upper Beaconsfield, Victoria, February 1983.* Technical Paper No. 3, National Centre for Rural Fire Research, Chisholm Institute of Technology, Caulfield East.

Loh E (2006) Centre for Risk and Community Safety, RMIT University.

Luke RH and McArthur AG (1977) *Bushfires in Australia.* Department of Primary Industry Forestry and Timber Bureau and CSIRO Division of Forest Research.

McCarthy GJ and Tolhurst KG (2001) Effectiveness of broad-scale fuel reduction burning in assisting with wildfire control in parks and forests in Victoria. Research Report No. 51.

Miller SI, Carter W and Stephens RG (1984) Report of the Bushfire Review Committee on bushfire disaster preparedness and response in Victoria, Australia, following the Ash Wednesday fires 16 February 1983.

Office of the Emergency Services Commissioner (2005) *Fire Refuges in Victoria Policy and Practice.* October.

Office of the Emergency Services Commissioner (2009),*Where are They Going? People Movement during Bushfires.* December.

Proudley M (2008) Fire, families and decisions. *Australian Journal of Emergency Management* **23** (1), 37–43.

Ramsay C (1983) Senior Principal Research Scientist, CSIRO Division of Building Research. Personal communication.

Ramsay C (1985) How bushfires set houses alight: lessons from Ash Wednesday. *Ecos* **43**, 3–7.

Ramsay C and Rudolph L (2003) *Landscape and Building Design for Bushfire Areas.* CSIRO Publishing, Melbourne.

Rhodes A (2009) Witness statement to 2009 Victorian Bushfires Royal Commission. WIT.3004.002.0001.

Shire of Yarra Ranges and Country Fire Authority, Victoria *Property Bushfire Preparation and Native Vegetation Management.* Case Study 1. TEN.179.001.

Slijepcevic A, Tolhurst KG, Saunder G, Whight S and Marsden-Smedley J (2007) A prescribed burning risk assessment tool. Presentation at AFAC Conference. September, Hobart.

Standards Australia *AS 3959-2009 Construction of Buildings in Bushfire-prone Areas.*

State Coroner Victoria (1999) 1997 Dandenong Ranges fires: inquest into the deaths of Jennifer Lindroth, Graham Lindroth and Genevieve Erin during a fire at Ferny Creek and four other fires in the Dandenong Ranges on 21 January 1997. Coronial Services Centre, Melbourne.

Sullivan A (2009) Research Scientist, Bushfire Behaviour and Management Group, CSIRO. Personal communication, email 30 October.

Thompson D (2006) Storing collections in high bushfire risk areas. History Victoria e-news no. 4, July. Based on information from Kim Morris of Art & Archival, Queanbeyan, and *A Burning Issue*, AICCM Victorian Division.

Tolhurst K (2009) Centre for Australian Weather and Climate Research, Attachment: Evidence of Fire Behaviour, Resp 3000.005.0240. Transcript, 21 May 2009, 2009 Victorian Bushfires Royal Commission.

Victorian Bushfires 2009 Research Taskforce (2009) Victorian 2009 Bushfire Research Response Interim Report. June. Bushfire CRC, RMIT University, Melbourne.

Victorian Building Commission (2009) *A Guide to Building in Victoria after the Bushfires.* Victorian Building Commission, Melbourne.

Victorian Education Department, Outer Eastern Metropolitan Region (1988) *Code of Practice for Schools in Fire Hazard Areas for Fire Protection of School Grounds.* DEECD, Melbourne.

Victorian Education Department, Outer Eastern Metropolitan Region (1989) *Code of Building Practice for Schools in Fire Hazard Areas.* DEECD, Melbourne.

Webster J (2000) *The Complete Bushfire Safety Book.* Random House, Sydney.

Whittaker J, Elliot G, Gilbert J, Handmer J, Haynes K, McLennan J and Cowlishaw S (2009) Human behaviour and community safety. Bushfire CRC, RMIT University, Melbourne.

Acknowledgements

For this updated 3rd edition, my very special thanks to Dr Andrew Sullivan, CSIRO's Senior Research Scientist and Research Group Leader, Bushfire Dynamics and Applications, for his invaluable assistance with incorporating the latest understandings of fire behaviour, and for other helpful suggestions on the text. Particular warm appreciation to Phil Cheney, former Director, National Bushfire Research Unit, CSIRO who wrote the Foreword, for not only contributing the benefit of his world-renowned expertise to the new chapter, *Township Protection*, but for his support over many years and ever-ready availability to answer my questions and check my interpretation of the facts; and to David Packham, OAM, honorary senior research fellow, Monash University School of Geography and Environmental Science, for access to their jointly-authored paper *Don't Mention the Fu.. Word!*

I am indebted to Professor John Handmer, Principal Scientific Adviser at the Bushfire Centre for Risk and Community, and Damien Killalea AFSM, Director, Community Fire Safety, Tasmania Fire Service, for taking the time to verify my interpretation of their post-Black Saturday research, *Review of fatalities in the February 7, 2009, bushfires, Final Report*, prepared with Saffron O'Neil for the Victorian Bushfires Royal Commission April 2010.

Appreciation also to Dr Kevin Tolhurst, Dept of Forest and Ecosystem Science, University of Melbourne and to Alan Rhodes, Manager Community Safety Research and Evaluation, Country Fire Authority, Victoria, both of whom kindly responded with answers and data; and to all those bushfire scientists whose research, as listed in the bibliography, has been invaluable.

This small book could not have been created without its mother publication, *The Complete Bushfire Safety Book* (Random House, 2000). So it is appropriate to give acknowledgement here for the cooperation of all rural fire, police and emergency services throughout Australia during my research and writing of it, for their reviewing of pertinent sections and their confidence in my work. The same for scientists of the CSIRO, in particular Phil Cheney, Director, National Bushfire Research Unit, and Dr Caird Ramsay,

Director, and Neville McArthur, Senior Research Officer of the Division of Building Research. And bushfire researchers Andrew A.G. Wilson and David Packham, who have a special interest and expertise in the problems of evacuation. To David Packham belongs the credit for the origin of the idea of an inbuilt refuge room (Chapter 11). My thanks also to the Fire Protection Association Australia. And officers of a multitude of government departments, including Agriculture, Natural Resources and the Environment, Victoria and the Commonwealth Bureau of Meteorology.

Their initial help, of course, underlies the accuracy of advice in this book.

A special thank you to my ever-helpful daughter Claire Seppings who made time from her extremely busy life to comment on aspects of the text; and to my friends Ann Quinton and Jillian Smith for applying their own considerable talents for word use to suggestions on the text and with it their ever-available frankness and patience with my obsessive perfectionism. Underpinning Ann's help was her own interest in bushfire safety. As a young mother with six very young children, Ann saw her own home destroyed during the Victorian bushfires of 1962.

For their enthusiasm about the worth of *Essential Bushfire Safety Tips*, their professional diligence in preparing and producing this edition, and being so easy to work with, my heart-felt thanks to David Holmgren, Su Dennett, Beck Lowe and all the staff at Melliodora Publishing.

About the author

Joan Webster OAM is an award-winning journalist who, since 1965, has written extensively on bushfire safety for the public.

She has observably done more than any other private individual to help make people and their homes safer during a bushfire. Her insights have been hailed as ground-breaking and her bushfire safety innovations become standard official recommendations. Her independent work on bushfire safety over almost 60 years, through articles, talks, broadcasts and books, earned her the Order of Australia Medal in 2010.

Joan Webster's pioneering *The Complete Australian Bushfire Book* (1986) caused a revolution in bushfire safety. It was republished in 2000 as *The Complete Bushfire Safety Book.* Acclaimed internationally by authorities and householders alike, it is acknowledged by bushfire and emergency services as the most authoritative publication of its type and considered the definitive work on bushfire safety for the householder. Emergency authorities and government departments throughout Australia use it as a resource, and bushfire services use it in the training of their officers.

Its in-depth analysis of the evacuation dilemma helped shape official policy. Safety concepts now accepted as basic, originally devised by Joan Webster and first made public in her book, include the personal Survival Kit; protective window shutters; special needs of children and the frail; care of pets; holiday safety; safety of precious possessions; the idea of preparing a family bushfire plan; and the step-by-step, logistical actions lists of what to do at various stages of bushfire threat.

For this ready reference, *Essential Bushfire Safety Tips*, Joan has distilled the understanding of bushfire behaviour, and the essence of bushfire dangers and safe reactions to them, dealt with in depth in her classic book.

Joan's interest in bushfire safety began young when at the age of 11, on her own initiative, she put out a backyard ignition that had been unnoticed by adults.

In 1964 she was a foundation member of the first municipal organisation for civil defence for bushfire, during which she gained many insights on the evacuate–stay problem. In 1987 *The Complete Australian Bushfire Book*, was short-listed for the BHP Pursuit of Excellence Award. In 1988, in recognition of her work on community refuges, she was appointed consultant to the Victorian Ministry of Education to advise on bushfire safety in schools. In 1989, her campaign for better bushfire safety for schools resulted in the Victorian Education Department's comprehensive Codes of Practice for Schools in bushfire-prone areas, and in the construction of the first purpose-built school bushfire refuges.

Her first profession was nursing. But for 25 years she was a newspaper reporter, investigative journalist, feature writer and crusader for many causes. The author of eight non-fiction, two fiction and 23 books of poetry, she has been widely published in print, radio, stage and television: in Australian folk history, biography, drama, children's stories, teenage fiction, satire, poetry and lyrics, ancient history and mythology, receiving strong reviewer and reader acclaim.

In 1990 she received the Australian Fire Protection Association's Community Service Award. In 2010 she received the Order of Australia *'For service to the community in raising awareness of bushfire safety'*.

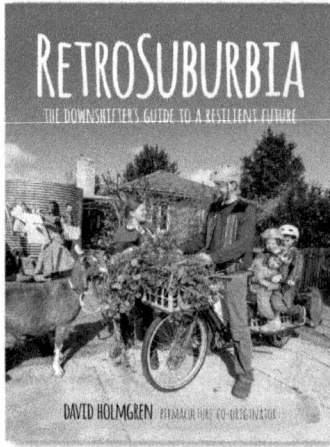

RetroSuburbia:
The downshifter's guide to a resilient future

by David Holmgren

From the co-originator of permaculture, this 592 page manual shows how Australians can downshift and retrofit their lives, homes and gardens to be more sustainable and resilient. It promises a challenging but exciting mix of satisfying work, a more meaningful way of living, and hope for the next generation as we move towards an uncertain future.

The book recognises bushfire preparedness as a key part of household resilience, with the chapters 'Retrofitting for bushfire defence' and 'Household disaster planning'. These chapters are also available as a downloadable pdf at retrosuburbia.com/reading

For more visit RetroSuburbia.com

The Flywire House:
A case study in design against bushfire

by David Holmgren

Providing a unique case study approach, The Flywire House offers design solutions for bushfire resilient building. Originally published in 1991, this classic book has been reprinted and is still compatible with latest understandings. A new foreword reviews the material in the context of the devastating 2009 'Black Saturday' bushfires in Victoria, Australia.

Available at holmgren.com.au

Further writings by David Holmgren on the topic of bushfire resilience and preparedness can be found at holmgren.com.au/bushfire

About the publisher

Melliodora Publishing was started by Su Dennett and her partner David Holmgren, co-originator of permaculture, to produce books and other media to support people in their permaculture journey, while bypassing the traditional gatekeepers of the publishing industry.

We aim to minimise adverse environmental impacts of the whole book creation, including printing, logistics and marketing chain, while providing a fair share return to authors, illustrators, editors and other creative contributors to the publishing process. We operate outside of monopolistic distribution and marketing systems of online conglomerates, and preference printing with owner-operated businesses in Australia and/or other markets rather than globalised corporations.

At all times we are guided by permaculture ethics and principles.

MELLI◯DORA
PUBLISHING

For more see melliodora.com

For more on permaculture see permacultureprinciples.com
For more on David Holmgren see holmgren.com.au;
for his take on possible climate change futures
see futurescenarios.org;
and for his practical strategies for a resilient future
see retrosuburbia.com

www.ingramcontent.com/pod-product-compliance
Lightning Source LLC
Chambersburg PA
CBHW072131020426
42334CB00018B/1753